RUTHLESS PREDATORS

Miscreants in the Workplace and How to Deal with Them

BY JAKE HAGERMAN

 FriesenPress

One Printers Way
Altona, MB R0G 0B0
Canada

www.friesenpress.com

ISBN
978-1-03-919427-4 (Hardcover)
978-1-03-919426-7 (Paperback)
978-1-03-919428-1 (eBook)

1. PSYCHOLOGY, INDUSTRIAL & ORGANIZATIONAL PSYCHOLOGY

Distributed to the trade by The Ingram Book Company

Table of Contents

PREFACE

My name is Jake Hagerman—a pseudonym actually. I'm recently retired from spending fifty years in the field of mental health services. The following book is meant for general reading by the lay public. Hence, I have tried to stay clear of professional vernacular that would sound too esoteric (do you get my drift?). In plain language, it provides a risk analysis, identifying and providing options to survive the "games played" by an organization miscreant, the term I've assigned to a ruthless predator located across all fields of employment, including entry level personnel, mid and senior management, board membership etcetera—this is a FACT, take it to the bank! The organizational miscreant is a ruthless predator with parasitic features, with a personality composed of four factors: narcissism (extreme self-indulgence); sadistic features both emotional and/or physical in presentation; lack of empathy (a limited capacity to understand or care about another person's feelings); and machiavellian behavior (i.e., back stabbing). Statements (Clarke, 2005) made during the past twenty plus years in industrial organization research indicate that approximately one in one hundred individuals in the general population are psychopathic. But more to the point, Babiak & Hare (2019) stated that of 203 high-potential executives in a research study, "about 3.9 percent fit the profile of the psychopath as measured on the PCL-R" (p.184). This is twice greater than 1 percent of the general population, and most businesses would be concerned upon learning this statistic.

In this book, I hesitate to use the term *psychopath,* with the public's inclination to conflate psychopathy with Charles Manson's diagnostic presentation and histrionic behavior in the American courtrooms. I suggest you obtain more information on the subject by reviewing the experts research findings identified in the following pages. This should provide a solid foundation of information pertaining to this book's analysis of human treachery on the part of the organization miscreant.

Throughout the book, I prefer to use the term "organization miscreant" whose presentation of behavior has its own unique features as disturbing and potentially dangerous as other subtypes of psychopathy, but distinctly different.[1]

Two of my previous books—*Love Your Enemies in Case Your Friends Turn Out To Be Bastards* (2012) and *Sharks, Slimeballs And Malcontents: Organizational Survival Guide* (2022)—describe aspects of working with and survival against the organization miscreant. In this book, the vignettes provided in Chapter Three are a series of anecdotes experienced by colleagues, acquaintances, and, last but not least, me. Of note: I have tried to portray the behaviors described as accurately as I can remember.

Nevertheless, I will let you be the judge of the honesty quotient of the various behaviors stated in the fifteen vignettes. Hopefully the dreadful extremity of "way-out-there abuse" described in these vignettes has *not* been experienced by you, but then again, I can't be naïve and presume you've lived and experienced a pristine work environment.

In the book, I have chosen the "Psychopathy Spectrum Test" to be used by lay people to assess the identified behavior of the organization miscreant. This test later provides experts additional information, prior to a much more in-depth assessment of the individual. This allows a logical progression of evaluation steps which includes hiring external experts (e.g., forensic psychiatrist, forensic psychologist) to evaluate the organization miscreant's behavior more thoroughly on site.

I suggest the following procedures should be attempted by the external experts: Using professional interviews with staff, the organization miscreant, and family members of both the identified perpetrator and the staff member(s) to assess the degree of trauma they

---

1   You will find considerable redundancy throughout the book which I purposely included to help reinforce the nature and behavior you need to be aware of to survive the organization miscreant's treachery and ruthless tenacity!

have received. This behavior—identified by the staff members as deeply inappropriate professional transgressions, with collateral damage—impacts the organization almost from the start of the miscreant's employment! Lastly, one must consider the secondary trauma to respective family members as a result of the continuous harassment and other deviant ploys against the loved one. All of which has caused emotional and physical suffering to the family unit! The greatest impact and accuracy with the process just described requires "action planning" by the staff, to allow cross referencing of the miscreant's behavior.

This information, supported by more detailed analysis from trained professionals, provides systematic evidence to help corroborate an accurate diagnosis of the aberrant behavior observed with the organization miscreant. The results are then described in detail by the expert clinicians; they include subsequent recommendations to management. The intended outcome is *expulsion* of this conniving individual from their respective positions of employment within the organization. That's the plan, but senior management has to be in agreement with the plan and have confidence in its final outcome. Believe it or not, that can be a problem, all of which is discussed in later chapters.

Tough approach, you think? Easy answer! The organization miscreant's behavior must be addressed—sooner, *not* later! This must be done to reduce the psychological damage to the employees of the organization and to uphold the organization's reputation! This psychological damage can create chaos for the recipient of inappropriate behavior (often daily) and danger to the dispirited staff in toto. This is emphatically stated, for with passage of time, the organization miscreant will wreak such havoc that the exiting staff will most assuredly down-grade the organization to their colleagues in the new job!

That's it, I hope you're primed for the following one hundred plus pages, now on to Chapter One.

CHAPTER ONE:

Behavioral Symptoms of the Organization Miscreant

I have been hesitant until now to provide a detailed overview of my professional background, the major reason being the potential for legal action taken by one or more of the individuals described in the subsequent vignettes. More specifically, if they were to find out their behavior was described in a published book and take legal action for one cause (such as defamation) or another—it's anyone's guess—they would most certainly pitch their innocence from all angles.

I would *not* put it past any one of the fifteen vignette representatives to respond aggressively! Don't worry, I can defend all information I or others witnessed in all cases provided in the vignettes. But—and it's a big but—we are dealing with a dishonorable person without integrity, who is vindictive as hell, often ready to pounce on any opportunity to respond in a malicious, cold-blooded manner, no quarter given—I hope I make my point! They worship power and control—at your expense!

Organization miscreants are dangerous, totally devoid of old fashioned humanity, lacking remorse, and highly narcissistic. In conjunction, they are always primed for any action to be taken, at which time they administer a cadre of "cruelty techniques" to defeat you at all costs. This pattern of vindictive behavior has been described in many texts as *malignant narcissism*. As a consequence, I VERY carefully researched, and chose the candidates depicted in this book, disregarding other potential candidates for the following reason. Most often the rejected candidate did *not* definitively reflect the criteria. That is, their presentation was *subclinical* in symptomatology, not matching the profile in the DSM V TR classification (2022, p. 885) and other professional expert opinions that I respect (e.g., Cleckley, 1976; Babiak, 1995; Levenson, Kiehl & Fitzpatrick, 1995; Clarke, 2005; Simon, 2010; Dutton, 1998, 2012; Hare, 2006, 2019).[2]

In sum, the organization miscreant is dangerous for your mental health, means of earning a living, and professional reputation. Let's move on, shall we.

My own experience includes working in four psychiatric institutions during the past fifty years, qualifying in both industrial-organization psychology and clinical psychology, an associate fellowship in one country and full fellowship in another, forty-two peer-reviewed publications, six published books, and lastly, both mid and senior management positions in the field of mental health during a twenty-year period.

In Clarke's book *Working with Monsters: How to Identify and Protect Yourself from the Workplace Psychopath* (2005), he makes a valid distinction (pp.26-27) between the antisocial personality disorder which describes a persistent *maladaptive behavioral pattern* that occurs across the lifespan (i.e., sociopath). He then states: "Psychopathy, on the other hand, refers to a *syndrome of personality and behavioural* characteristics," and suggests the syndrome is caused by "psychological, biological, genetic and social factors *rather than social factors alone*." In this regard, Dr. Clarke has stated that "it is the unique combination of biological, genetic, and environmental factors that interact in a specific way to produce a psychopath" (p.56). He also states, "given that a number of different types of psychopaths that exist in the workplace (e.g., organizational psychopath, corporate criminal psychopath, violent criminal psychopath, and occupational psychopath) it seems logical that growing up in different environments leads to different types of psychopaths" (p.50).

---

2   Subclinical behavior is not severe enough to present definite or readily observable symptoms.

Having worked with the four subtypes of psychopaths in my career I would also endorse Dr. Clarke's observation that there are common characteristics of *all* psychopaths. More specifically, four personality traits called the "Dark Tetrad" which include:

- Highly narcissistic tendencies;
- Lack of empathy;
- Machiavellian behavior (i.e., backstabbing, vindictive behavior); and
- Sadism—this one proposed more recently (i.e., enjoyment of hurting others, either/both emotional and physical sadistic behavior).

Organization miscreants scoring high on the Dark Tetrad certainly display the fourth trait mentioned above; don't overlook their tendency on the job site to be both overtly and covertly sadistic with a capital S! These four personality characteristics, when played out in the workplace, inevitably cause severe damage to the infrastructure of the organization, and most certainly cause damage on a personal level with the cruel and often antagonistic interactions imposed on subordinates, peers, and superiors.

Moshagen, Hilbig, and Zettler (2018) have suggested that all dark personalities (i.e., Dark Tetrad) have as their core (D): "A general tendency toward ethically, morally, and/or socially questionable behavior" and further state, "D is the basic tendency to maximize one's utility at the expense of others." This certainly describes the behavior I've witnessed by subclinical psychopaths as well.

Of note: People with primary psychopathy tend to be defective in *all situations* because of (D) mentioned above. The statement by Moshagen et al is supported by Matthew Gervais, a Canadian researcher at Simon Fraser University who describes individuals with subclinical levels of the Dark Tetrad, where some criteria are met but not enough to achieve clinical status. In other words, these individuals are experiencing symptoms at a subthreshold level that are *not* severe enough or persistent enough to merit a diagnosis of psychopathy. In the context of organization manipulation techniques, those individuals identified as subclinical are prone to use strategic exploitation of others, choosing to co-operate in situations when it will maximize their intentions (i.e., the end justifies the mean mentality). I would suggest this encapsulates the description of sociopathy.

In conjunction, Clarke (2005) has discussed at length in Chapter Four of his book the following characteristics of the organization miscreant: manipulative organizational behavior; unethical behavior; intolerance/easily bored; unpredictable behavior/shallow emotions; parasitic behavior; undependable/failure to take responsibility for behavior; workplace bullying; seeking increased power and control in the company; creating conflict between organization members; interpersonal behavior: deceitful/devious/frequent lying/intimidating behavior.

These characteristics are substantiated by Babiak and Hare (2019, pp.254-262) when they provide red flags to consider, such as: inability to form a team; inability to share; disparate treatment of staff; inability to tell the truth; inability to be modest; inability to accept blame; inability to act consistently and predictably; inability to react calmly; inability to act without aggression.

It would be advantageous for you to review in more depth these various behaviors discussed in the Clarke (2005) and Babiak et al (2019) resources to expand your knowledge of identified problematic behavior of organization miscreants. This allows you to begin making some preliminary observations regarding the "range of continuum" with which your identified individual falls. This continuum has subclinical presentation at the lower end to primary (i.e., full) presentation of symptoms at the higher end, based on the consistency and degree of problematic behavior observed. It never hurts to start logging such behavior to be used as evidence later on!

CHAPTER TWO:

Psychopathy Spectrum Test

Evaluating the Organization Miscreant

At this point you're probably wondering: *What can we do as a group of disgruntled staff within our working environment!?* The answer, whether employed in a union shop or not, is providing DATA to the "higher ups" regarding this individual's pathological behavior! In plain English, furnishing senior management with a profile of unprofessional conduct which reflects a colleague's deeply disturbing tendency to chronically devalue other people and by this tendency, erode the organization's efficiency and effectiveness. The profiling process completed by well-meaning staff members is an aid to navigate the investigation process to the best advantage of the organization. It can also be used by senior management to rationalize hiring expert clinicians to further evaluate the individual in question. This process sounds easy, however, please be aware that the political repercussions of "troubleshooting" comes into play, as many board members are wary of any potential "fallout" that might occur (e.g., lawsuits). This I observed on frequent occasions throughout my career.

Of note: If the organization miscreant is a union member, they will often use any/all means at their discretion to extend, manipulate, and corrupt the investigation process evaluating their ruthless conduct. This is an important point to remember. The organization miscreant has carefully learned the intricacies of the policy and procedure manual to increase their ability to finesse the system. At that point, the games played can become dirty and underhanded, perpetration is at full RAM speed, no prisoners taken! I have, over many years of employment in the mental health industry, been entangled in no less than a half dozen scenarios wherein the vengeful behavior by the organization miscreant escalated to such a degree that City, County and/or Federal authorities were thrust into the mix! I have described a number of these experiences in the vignettes provided in the next chapter.

As a suggestion, the instrument I feel would be appropriate to collect quantitative data as a collateral source for your defense and part of your risk analysis, is called the "Psychopathy Spectrum Test" (IDR-PST Labs, 2022). This evaluation tool is the property of IDR-PST Labs International which used Levenson's research (1995), but is not associated with Levenson's assessment instrument entitled, "Levenson Self-Report Psychopathy Test. The Psychopathy Spectrum Test has administrative utility, validity, and capabilities for use by lay people to identify the range of psychopathic behavior. More specifically, biol./ psychol./social integration which includes; psychopathic, sociopathic (behavioral delinquency), impulsive, and normal behavior. The quantitative data is measured in four quadrants labeled *psychopathic, sociopathic, impulsive behavior, normal.*

This assessment instrument can be completed by a cadre of staff, regardless of level of authority, and *prior to* contracting qualified experts in forensic psychology and/or forensic psychiatry. Of note: forensic psychologists are qualified in psychometric evaluation (psychological testing) which provides important data across a number of presenting symptoms reflected in the Dark Tetrad.

The Psychopathy Spectrum Test's basic use is to provide baseline information from a group of colleagues who are very knowledgeable of the organization miscreant's conduct/presenting behavior in the work milieu, and also personal information about their past and current family life. In point of fact, in all vignette cases (i.e., Chapter Three) the personal history of each candidate became well known. The information collected provides data for the contracted forensic expert(s) to review when they start their subsequent investigation, if and when that occurs. If not, it provides quantified information for the executive board and/or union investigators to support "getting the ball rolling" towards eventual dismissal procedures. As previously mentioned, the union should be involved from the outset of the evaluation procedures. Unfortunately, I've seen the evolution of their professional input "go south" in many circumstances, for no other reason than they were simply outclassed by this deviant and very corrupt individual. Further comments about that in Chapter Four.

The quantitative data from the Psychopathy Spectrum Test also provides additional information to support the staff's verbal/written complaints and as mentioned, *prior* to recommending to senior management hiring qualified experts for further in-depth assessment/diagnosis. Which may include utilizing the B-Scan 360 assessment instrument described at the end of Chapter 5. The management should benefit from receiving both qualitative data (i.e., personal complaints) from an array of company personnel, and quantitative data, using a *validated* assessment instrument(s) evaluating "across the board" the miscreant's presenting behavior assessed by the same cadre of employees. The completion of both types of evaluation methods reduces error rate in the complaint process and increases the credibility of staff action regarding the organization miscreant. It also provides quantitative baseline information to be analyzed by the contracted forensic expert(s) prior to the commencement of their clinical evaluation.

How to Successfully Implement the Psychopathy Spectrum Test

Below, I have developed a step-by-step process to organize and complete the Psychopathy Spectrum Test successfully, both on an individual basis and then on a collective basis, after collating the data from the designated cadre of complainants.

Preamble

The following information provides a "gateway" for the use of this assessment instrument. The Psychopathy Spectrum Test originated from research data which was initially developed by Levenson, Kiehl & Fitzpatrick in 1995. Subsequently, IDR-PST Lab International incorporated the data to formulate the instrument we currently use. Of note: the Psychopathy Spectrum Test is *not* to be mistaken for the Levenson Self-Report Psychopathy Scale. The former test is validated for measuring a person's degree of psychopathy and has also been used to evaluate psychopathic traits in non-institutional people. It is listed on the internet (https://www.idrlabs.com/psychopathy-spectrum/test.php) and provides an easy-to-follow process by completing twenty-seven questions such as, "Do you have psychopathic tendencies? For each of the following questions indicate how well it applies to you or the person you are evaluating."

Step One

The test has five pictorials after each question, which are a continuum of pictures from thumbs down to thumbs up. Choose the one that best reflects the way you assess yourself, and later on repeat the process regarding the organization miscreant's behavior. Completing this test is *not* a difficult task and should take less than thirty minutes.

Questions – Psychopathy Spectrum Test

1. I let others worry about so-called "higher values"; my main concern is to get what I want.
2. I end up in the same kinds of trouble, time after time.
3. I quickly lose interest in the tasks I start.
4. Looking out for myself is my top priority.

5. Before I do anything, I carefully consider the possible consequence.
6. People who get ripped off usually deserve it.
7. I am often bored.
8. I have never been in trouble with the law.
9. I would be upset if my success came at someone else's expense.
10. Even if I were trying very hard to sell something, I wouldn't lie to get my way.
11. I feel justified doing whatever I can to succeed.
12. Love is overrated.
13. I feel bad when my words or actions cause someone else emotional pain.
14. I find that I am able to pursue one goal for a long time.
15. Cheating isn't justified, because it's unfair to others.
16. When I get frustrated, I get very angry very quickly.
17. I have been in a lot of shouting matches with people.
18. I tell other people what they want to hear so that they will do what I want them to do.
19. I make a point of trying not to hurt others in pursuit of my goals.
20. I don't plan anything very far in advance.
21. Success is about the survival of the fittest; I am not concerned about losers.
22. My main purpose in life is getting as many good things as I can.
23. Making a lot of money is one of my most important goals.
24. What's right is whatever I can get away with.
25. I enjoy manipulating other people's feelings.
26. Most of my problems are due to the fact that other people don't understand me.
27. I sometimes find myself admiring a really clever scam.

Step Two

After completing the test, the instrument provides a score in each of four quadrants (a square divided into four sections). Each section is labelled as follows:

- upper left side: *sociopath*
- upper right side: *psychopath*
- lower left side: *normal*
- lower right side *impulsive.*

Sociopath	Psychopath
Normal	Impulsive

Your final score will appear inside one of the four quadrants, with a qualifier statement as to the percentage you obtained regarding the amount of the specific trait you reflected in your answers for each quadrant. Definitions are provided at the end of the Psychopathy Spectrum Test for each of the four traits: psychopathic, sociopathic, impulsive, normal. This is done to provide greater focus on the specific characteristics of each trait while examining the respective individual's presenting behavior described in each vignette.[3,4]

Step Three

This is an important step in the process of developing a group evaluation of the miscreant's behavior as a *team strategy* to complete the

---

3   Please read the vignettes carefully, scoring the definitions of each trait from the twenty-seven questions that match the identified behavior of the organization miscreant.

4   You will notice that in the writer's assessment of the fifteen vignette candidates at the end of the book, *no one* scored in the "normal" quadrant. This reflects the extremity of the behavior demonstrated by the fifteen individuals and their degree of emotional disturbance relative to the general population.

Psychopathy Spectrum Test. **This is done after you have exhausted all attempts to alert management of the organization miscreant's ongoing deviant and very destructive behavior!**

I cannot emphasize this point enough. The group evaluation is completed AFTER you have permission from senior management, or have hit a road block in seeking and *not* receiving meaningful support from the "higher ups" in management. In their defense, they are often targeted by the miscreant after being thoroughly evaluated by this person and then cleverly deceived. In some cases, they are blackmailed with regard to past failed requests by the organization miscreant for management to meet the miscreant's personal/professional agenda. Recent political behavior in various international organizations can attest to the "skullduggery" used by the organization miscreant when provoked.

In this situation, management will often be hesitant to initiate any action that would arouse vindictive behavior; in essence, they are held at ransom (i.e., legal action; media attention). However, if the working environment is *not* a union shop, what choice do you have? In my experience in these situations, the ship is already listing, soon to sink, unless aggressive action is taken.

Let's be crystal clear about what I'm suggesting. I am *not* condoning unethical behavior, such as clandestine maneuvers. But occasionally the "final straw" behavior by management's refusal to intervene effectively requires drastic action by the underlings, or the ship will not just list, but sink to the murky depths below. I've seen this occur on frequent occasions (identified in the vignettes found in Chapter 3). If your group of "take action" colleagues is cohesive and ready to commence an organized, carefully thought-out rescue mission, they should benefit from reading the following action steps. **It is your choice to take action or not; carefully weigh the pros and cons of your final decision in this matter.**

Action Steps

a. PRIVATELY organize a meeting *outside of working hours* with like-minded colleagues who are fed up with a lack of effective action by management. To momentarily digress, in one situation I personally encountered, the organization miscreant was allowed a free hand, getting away with her emotional brutalizing of the staff for twenty-six months! This continued even after many (ten plus) *formal* attempts by staff to alert the board of directors to the ongoing catastrophic effect this individual was having on the organization. This form of "emotional vandalism" by the miscreant is described in detail in Chapter 4.

b. Each team member should complete the Psychopathy Spectrum Test to obtain a score on themselves and subsequently complete the test again, replacing "I" with the miscreant's pronoun. This time, assess the organization miscreant's behavior and obtain a result in the four quadrants. Why complete the test by each team member on themselves, you ask? To see if anyone is an outlier—falling beyond the "Normal" quadrant—is one answer. If so, their presence could be identified as a major bias and negative influence during the final collation of the data by the team as a whole and used by the miscreant's legal defense in a court case.

c. After collating each of the scores from the respective team members and examining the results, you will probably find the organization miscreant's final collated score falls in either the sociopathic or psychopathic quadrant. If it doesn't, the miscreant could still be in the subclinical range (as defined earlier) and is capable of deviant, obstructive behavior in the future. In essence, their behavior is still skewed in comparison with the general population by possessing the "D" Dark Tetrad, yet stays below the surface of clinical detection. In other words, some criteria might be met but not enough to achieve a primary clinical status, however, this may increase to primary status in the future, depending on the conditions.

d. Develop an ongoing "working report," which with time and refinement (several reviews) becomes a highly explicit exposé of the facts regarding the organization miscreant's destructive behavior throughout the work milieu in toto. The report becomes a lay benchmark for future perusal by the management if they choose to make recommendations to hire the previously discussed expert(s) to complete a more in-depth clinical/forensic evaluation. As an aside:

Repercussions by senior management suggesting insubordinate behavior by the clandestine group, who operated *without* formal approval of this evaluation process should *not* be trivialized! More specifically, if the organization miscreant has "caught wind" of this operation, they can intervene with the senior management and impose a highly convincing counter argument cloaked in cunning deceit and inuendo.

a. At this point, what could be described as final straw territory, the funding bodies of the organization are contacted, if they haven't been already, to intervene and make demands on the board to aggressively act to rectify the problem! If not, the organization, with time, will probably deteriorate, and the miscreant will move on to their next job opportunity. I was personally involved in one of these disastrous situations; fortunately, the board was aggressively urged to terminate the organization miscreant before eventual ruin.

CHAPTER THREE:

Vignettes

Let's take a breather for a few minutes and let me "free associate" with some important information pertaining to the evolution of the organization miscreant's presenting behavior.

While reviewing a book by Dutton (1998), I noticed a section that describes the development of organization miscreants with some important background information to keep in mind. I felt this was a necessary and important precursor before you read the following fifteen vignettes (short stories) of "skewed" and very delinquent behavior within an organization. After which, you will have the opportunity to personally evaluate the conduct described, using the Psychopathy Spectrum Test and subsequently compare your results with the writer's. So here goes.

A child's attachment to abusive parents, the child's primary caregivers, is a source of pain and misery! Not a great leap in logic, but here's the problem. The RAGE that is experienced by the child can be seriously repressed and its expression distorted because of such delinquent parenting, until a similar intimate attachment is formed later in life.

Specifically, according to Dutton, the child's underlying personality will remain dormant until an intimate attachment later in life "triggers" the emotional template developed in the original attachment experience. The upshot being, abusive people physically abused in their family of origin are at risk for ambivalent attachment. As well, a faulty internal model, particularly self-concepts and expectations of attachment to other people, are fraught with rage and fear. These ingredients are the basic groundwork for abusive behavior to present itself in interpersonal relationships. In essence, *abusive relationships predict learned behavior patterns in the future*, as they influence avoidant-ambivalent bonding styles that generate tendencies which are excessively demanding and angry in adult attachments.

In other words, one could also state that the organization miscreant's behavior is a re-enactment of developmental problems compounded by a biological predisposition and familial dysfunction in their formative years that is generalized (played out) in adulthood. I hope I didn't lose anyone in this description by Dutton; let's proceed, shall we.

The Training Approach

In the following section, I suggest you study in detail each vignette's story-line with the expressed purpose of evaluating the behavior using the Psychopathy Spectrum Test found on the internet. The breadth and depth of each vignette provides enough "practice effect" (repetition of behavior) to initiate a feeling of comfort using this evaluation instrument. This approach, as a training tool, provides a formal template of information from which to base your observations of Dark Tetrad behaviors.

Prior to commencing this exercise, once again, please review the following presenting behavior you will find on the Internet to *increase* your critical thinking skills for each vignette!

Questions – Psychopathy Spectrum Test

1. I let others worry about so-called "higher values"; my main concern is to get what I want.
2. I end up in the same kinds of trouble, time after time.
3. I quickly lose interest in the tasks I start.

4. Looking out for myself is my top priority.
5. Before I do anything, I carefully consider the possible consequence.
6. People who get ripped off usually deserve it.
7. I am often bored.
8. I have never been in trouble with the law.
9. I would be upset if my success came at someone else's expense.
10. Even if I were trying very hard to sell something, I wouldn't lie to get my way.
11. I feel justified doing whatever I can to succeed.
12. Love is overrated.
13. I feel bad when my words or actions cause someone else emotional pain.
14. I find that I am able to pursue one goal for a long time.
15. Cheating isn't justified, because it's unfair to others.
16. When I get frustrated, I get very angry very quickly.
17. I have been in a lot of shouting matches with people.
18. I tell other people what they want to hear so that they will do what I want them to do.
19. I make a point of trying not to hurt others in pursuit of my goals.
20. I don't plan anything very far in advance.
21. Success is about the survival of the fittest; I am not concerned about losers.
22. My main purpose in life is getting as many good things as I can.
23. Making a lot of money is one of my most important goals.
24. What's right is whatever I can get away with.
25. I enjoy manipulating other people's feelings.
26. Most of my problems are due to the fact that other people don't understand me.
27. I sometimes find myself admiring a really clever scam.

Vignette 1: Sven

One particular individual I knew from the early-late 1970s called Sven, had arrived from Scandinavia a few years prior. Looking back at our first meeting, after a few beers he stated he was the strongest man in the city (population 400,000). He started to discuss his background in detail; I beg your pardon, we had barely met! According to Sven, he had been a highly successful weightlifter in his earlier years (bronze medalist of Scandinavia), a martial arts practitioner (but refused to be graded to a higher belt level—in two different martial arts), and was a dedicated "lady's man" while still unhappily married. He further stated he had enrolled in university part-time and would be studying philosophy. His training in the automotive trade was completed in Scandinavia; at one point he described a physical wrestling match with a student rival at his lodgings. Basically, his arm was held down on top of a hot stove element—he still bore a third-degree burn scar. This he showed me and laughed it off.

All of the above information, during this first meeting, was disclosed in the space of three hours and many beers, paid by me. In future meetings, he often denigrated his mother's "crappy parenting" and rarely discussed his father. I observed that he HAD to be the center of attention in all social situations and that his eldest child, a brilliant fifteen-year-old male with significant math skills, had anger management problems with impulsive "hair trigger" outbursts. He openly conveyed contempt for his father, preferring to "hibernate in his room" as Sven used to say. His thirteen-year-old daughter was already "tough minded" and moderately confrontational towards Sven and condescending to her brother. Lastly, Sven's youngest male child, age eight, was quiet, saw his father as a hero, and tried to emulate his athletic feats in the backyard. His brother and sister didn't show interest and were never present. Sven was very critical of any errors his youngest son made during sporting activities, adopting an attitude of "do it my way or the highway." Tough love in these situations set a marked authoritarian tone throughout the household.

I observed over time that Sven prided himself in provoking diatribes (aggressive debates) and usually won because of his "philosophical training." His attitude towards his wife was aggressive, belittling, and condescending with a capital C. She retaliated but ineffectively due to her broken English and heavy accent, which he loved to ridicule. He often made late-night phone calls to his paramours, with his wife within earshot. When asked by myself—Sven at this time was in his mid-thirties –"What are you aspiring to be at this point in your career?" (he was currently employed as an autobody tradesman), he stated in a matter-of-fact, heavily accented voice, "I want to be a willage wise man!" Sven had difficulty pronouncing his v's. By this time, he had worked as a tradesman with automobiles in the daytime for several years, was completing a bachelor's degree in philosophy in the evening, and was a doorman/bouncer at the local university's graduate student lounge on the weekends.

Earlier in his career, he had achieved a commercial airline pilot training program (I saw a diploma that looked official). Of note: In his early twenties, he completed his Armed Forces training in Scandinavia (two-year conscription) and spent time soldiering in West Africa during a civil war period in several countries in the early 1960s. And lastly, he was an accomplished scuba diver, which he bragged about. More specifically, he bragged about the extreme depth he would challenge himself to reach, with an obvious risk to his life and a carefree manner about its effect on his health or his family's security.

Moving forward, at the time I knew him, his most famous line when he became enamored with a female was "If you don't want to fox me you can sax me off," which often invited sexual congress with his object of desire and potential conquest, or a quick rebuttal and rejection. But in Sven's words, "Jake, you try ten times, you score one." More to the point, one incident stands out in my mind almost fifty years later. I was in my early twenties and being "mentored" by Sven, this older Scandinavian man in his mid-thirties, bored with life, limited job prospects, supporting three children and a nagging, unforgiving spouse. To liven things up, he would "hustle" young coeds at the university after doing a handstand on a bar table. Yes, on the bar table, you got it right!! One night, while sitting at a table at the bar where Sven "bounced," I observed a beautiful, young blonde, approximately twenty-two years of age, wearing tight jeans that appeared spray-painted on, and a "no bra Friday" look, who ran up and gave him a big hug.

She proceeded to compliment Sven on his discussion at the tutorial group earlier that day and was so impressed that he was a committed Buddhist (yeah right!?). The young woman invited Sven back to her apartment "to discuss Buddhism philosophy." As Sven was leaving the bar, he looked over his shoulder at me and lifted his eyebrows quickly a couple of times with a sly smile. Sven was very adept at using his physique, accent, and European charm to seduce a great variety of women. As he would say, "Black ones, white ones, yellow ones, mixed race, no matter, Jake."

Later in the week, when we met up again, Sven, as usual, debriefed in very graphic detail, his liaison with this most recent conquest, which included his usual malapropisms: "I had two orgasmas and she really enjoyed oral general intercourse when I was spend." Apparently when they arrived at her apartment, she said she had to go to the bathroom for a few moments and would return eager to discuss Buddhism. Sven used this opportunity to strip naked in her living room and present a lovely big erection upon her return.

To digress, I visited Sven at his workplace several times and met his boss who, according to Sven, was defrauding work invoices to reduce taxable income. Sven decided to keep a copy of the exact work done on each vehicle, in case he needed what he stated was "protection money." In his words, "I am not stupid in the head!" If threatened with complicity, he believed his evidence would provide him sanctuary from any charges. I once observed Sven lift the back end of a Volkswagon bug off the ground, as he was too lazy to pick up the jack lying twenty feet away. He was that strong and loved to project his giant, male ego of power, strength, and indomitable spirit.

In the late 1970s, Sven decided to leave the city. Over the phone, he said to me, "I have decided to become a Willage Wiseman and will bicycle from Marseille to India. I do not correspond but say goodbye and hope you will not forget me." He left the city that week in April, 1978, and I haven't seen nor heard from him since.

I invite you to complete the Psychopathy Spectrum Test for Sven. When you have completed the test, compare your results with the author's test results at the back of the book under the heading "Author's Test Results – Fifteen Vignettes."

Vignette 2: Sharon: The Twenty-Year-Old Female Client

I was requested to complete a Social Assistance application for a young, single mother, who, as it turned out, was blonde, petite, and good looking, but, as I later discovered, had sinister motives and manipulative tendencies. I phoned the client prior to traveling to her downtown address, pre-arranging a time to meet. I was familiar with the case profile by this time. After six months on the job, I had encountered a great number of single mothers with children under five years of age. The innocent naiveté of the client's adolescent voice on the phone supported my preconception of who I thought I would encounter. How wrong was my presumption! When I got to the client's street and looked for the address number, I saw a young woman peer through a window from an apartment complex and then move quickly out of sight. I looked down at my day calendar, reaffirming that I had the right address, before getting out of my vehicle. I made a mental note to ask the applicant if she was currently seeking employment and was developing a job search list that I could review. A standard question asked in these circumstances. As I was to find out later on, this individual named Sharon, was very well versed in manipulating the system and had done so without effective intervention.

I knocked on the client's door, which was opened briskly, and there stood a twenty-year-old blonde, blue-eyed beauty dressed in tight-fitting jeans that highlighted a lovely, svelte figure. I couldn't believe how this woman got into those jeans, let alone was able to sit down without passing out, they were that tight. What was even more provocative was her T-shirt with the following inscription printed in dark, bold letters: I'LL GIVE HEAD TILL I'M DEAD. *Ummm, sounds like a set-up, Jake.* I was curious what her next ploy would be.

She invited me inside, and her walk, or should I say wiggle, from the doorway to the kitchen table was meant to impress. I sat down adjacent to her, opened my government valise and began taking out the application material while she sat staring at me intently with those large, blue eyes, going blink, blink, blink. I began to interview in the most professional voice I could muster. When I finished, she requested clarification on several points. Her voice, its cadence and relaxed manner, reflected someone who'd gone through this routine many, many times before. She was, I felt, very practiced at discerning strengths and weaknesses of the respective caseworkers who had taken her application in the past and then navigating them along a path that met her personal agenda. Twenty minutes later, this gut feeling was confirmed as I wondered who was interviewing whom! The picture on the sideboard in her living room showed her preschool son, approximately three years of age, being held by a good-looking, long-haired gentleman, with my client beside him in a stagnant, artificial pose. She noticed my eyes wandering around her apartment, and when I asked her about the current nature of her relationship, she stated rather calmly, nodding at the picture, "He's doing time in Federal prison."

I asked when he was due for parole, and she answered, "I'm not exactly sure. He's in for first-degree murder."

That set the tempo for the rest of our interview!!

My client acknowledged she was currently unemployed and showed a job search list and then stated she had not received any monies from an external source, indicating she was indigent, thereby making her technically eligible for Social Assistance. Next, I looked at her bank book and requested her taxation statement from the previous two years. This is when things went sideways 180 degrees and began to get seriously confrontational! My question and request, innocuous by any standard and required by my job, had caused a disconnect with the logical flow, or more precisely, her anticipated and premeditated, rehearsed diatribe.

Remember what I stated earlier that my gut told me I was dealing with a pro, and here I was once again about to be bitten in the proverbial rear end—big time! What occurred next was a vitriolic harangue from an AGGRESSIVE woman who was prepared to pull out all the stops to get her needs met, at my expense! Anger is putting it mildly; the rage caused, in her perception, by a flunky welfare worker trying to run the show—not on your life, I'm greatly pissed off scenario! Not a nice position to be put in. To reiterate, I'm stating her behavior went beyond the pale—not just a client losing their temper and giving a blast to release their frustration. Her anger went far beyond that level of anger; far, far beyond and with a potential to get REALLY ugly!

The behavioral escalation and threats of retaliation, both verbal (e.g., "I'll ride your ass to get what I deserve", " I know people who know people! Do you get my meaning Sir!!") continued to escalate to threats of legal action and personal intimidation. Within five minutes the writer wondered if she had gone off a medication regimen.

All of us have been in stressful situations, I'm sure you know what I'm talking about; your mouth becomes dry, and you start to lose confidence, composure, and articulation. The client's big blue eyes by this point were steady-state automatons. I'm talking HATRED in her gaze, no more seductive blink, blink, blink. Her eyes were riveted on me with an intense, focused stare—that cold-blooded, scary, 1000-yard stare! I imagined she had used this ploy as a conditioned response to intimidate, manipulate, and crush any opposition many times in the past! Instinctively I recoiled at her behavior and began to feel like mush. Quite frankly, size means nothing in these situations, and I was fully aware the client's behavior could "ratchet up" another 20-30 percent in intensity and potential violence. I was becoming cowed by this woman's conduct and started looking for avenues of escape. I sensed she intuitively felt my nerve was breaking, the will to survive compromised. I'm sure my facial expression gave away my insecurity.

IT GOT WORSE. There was a knock at the door and in walked a young man holding her beautiful three-year-old son in his arms, asking how things were going. This guy was a dead ringer for the late character actor Jack Palance, who in his day was one of the most intimidating Hollywood "heavies" from the early 1950s to late 1980s. In essence, the client's visitor looked a nasty piece of work. In hindsight, his sudden appearance out of nowhere was, I'm sure, orchestrated to maximize the threat imperative, and it worked! At this point I asked to use the client's kitchen phone to contact my supervisor regarding the application. In the late 1970s there were no cell phones; you had to use a normal land-line telephone. "No problem," both stated simultaneously; once again an eerie feeling crept over me that they'd done this schtik many, many times before!

Old Joe (his nickname), my supervisor, answered the phone. He was the epitome of the calm, reserved, reassuring Englishman. He was and had been for thirty years a perfect foil for this type of client behavior and asked about my problem. At this point, the Jack Palance look-alike "friend" picked up another phone in the living room to overhear our conversation. I stared at him, shrugged my shoulders, and asked, "Can I help you?" His response came as no surprise, and with absolutely no tact and amazing gall stated, "I pay the friggin' rent here, so I think I have the right to know what the hell's comin' down!" Not the best response if you want money from the government!?

That did it, my client WAS receiving financial support from an external source, and she had lied! This probably negated her eligibility for Social Assistance under the provisions of the welfare act, or at least would require a further inquiry about her financial circumstances. At this point, the Jack Palance look-alike and my client, had successfully accomplished their agenda to break my confidence and force, I can't think of another word, an abrogation of my responsibility to the taxpayer, or so they thought! In short their behavior had been finally challenged which caused a "meltdown". Their cunning deceit and aggressive ploys in the past had not worked this time. Please read on.

Thank God for the Old Joe's of the world; he had quickly surmised what was going on and requested my immediate return to the office, "to provide better service and one-to-one supervision regarding this very unique and complicated case." The Jack Palance look-alike started to blather about his rights being sullied, actually the preamble included F-words that ended with ING. The woman became unhinged, and for a microsecond I thought she was going to come across the kitchen table at me. I also believe if she had had a homemade "shank" in close vicinity, she would have used it on me. NO doubt in my mind.

My phone response to Old Joe being overheard was of course contrived and well-acted: "Joe, are you saying that you want me to leave? I'm sure we can sort things out here." His retort—"Get your ass back to the office NOW"—reaffirmed his boss-man authority and helped to mollify this very tense situation. I shrugged my shoulders, hung up the phone, put my application material back into my valise, and walked slowly out the door, feeling their eyes riveted on the back of my head. I then expected the Jack Palance look-alike to step in front of me as I left, or in some way impede my forward progress, which could have been interpreted as an assault under the criminal code of the country. I casually walked down the driveway towards my car and took time to quickly look over my shoulder. There stood the Jack Palance look-alike and my client holding her three-year-old son. Their staring, glaring, riveted gaze continued, and then both individuals moved away from the door and out of sight. As I type this paragraph, that image of them slowly moving out of sight reminds me of a film scene of a great white shark, mouth wide open, sinking slowly backwards from the camera into the dark depths of the ocean.

Lastly, as I remember, three words come to mind—MENACING, DANGEROUS, and then SAFETY a second later, when I got to my car and had a sudden urge to scream, urinate, vomit in that order. Eventually, when I returned to the office, a crowd had formed by the front door, led by Old Joe. Everyone shook my hand, congratulating my "retreat with honor," or more to the point "saving face for the office." That was the extent of the "psychologically healthy work place" support in those days. Nonetheless, it felt good to be received in this fashion. Unknown to me, two of my colleagues had had encounters with this pair over the past several years, enduring the same intimidation ploy that I had. One of them required two weeks of stress leave from work, so in my mind I had risen to the challenge and survived! By the way, Jack Palance's look-alike was in fact the brother of the client's partner—the one doing time in the pen for first-degree murder.

I invite you to complete the Psychopathy Spectrum Test for Sharon, the twenty-year-old female client. When you have completed the test, compare your results with the author's test resultsat the back of the book under the heading "Author's Test Results – Fifteen Vignettes."

Vignette 3: Joe: Administrator/Director/Autocrat

One morning, looking in the mirror before showering, I realized I was coming to the end of my frustration tolerance. My role of overseeing eight supervisors who routinely ganged up on me at our weekly meetings had exhausted me, and looking back, I don't blame them. My energy, stamina, and goal-directedness had diminished during the past twenty months under the sleight-of-hand, take-a-pounding management style of the not-so-new administrator/director/autocrat. At work a few days later, my phone rang with the extension number 57, and my hand trembled.

The sham male "sexy" voice was distinct. "I just want to say how enjoyable it's been working with you the past twenty months. I'd be interested to know your feelings on this matter?"

I almost fell out of my chair and bit my tongue before responding. *Here it comes.* "It has been an interesting and at times difficult twenty months, but here we are."

A pregnant pause for three one hundreds before he responded with, "Why don't you come down and spend some time with me, it appears we have to talk and clear the air."

My response, "How 'bout two p.m. this Thursday," was all I could muster.

"See you then," he said. The affectation, with a quiet, mellow tone or should I say "purr" was both disingenuous and seductive in his attempt to be disarming. But if you look at the meta-communication (i.e., hiding authentic self to gain increased social acceptance), a threat-imperative was there, most definitely there!

To top it off, not ten minutes later, at my staff meeting, I was provided with a list of complaints from the eight supervisors—all of whom had signed a letter of non-confidence regarding my management ability and leadership. *UNBELIEVABLE*, I thought to myself!! What I'd done for their survival, shielding them nine out of ten times from this idiot's illogical demands, reckless and contrived directives that appeared to make sense but didn't make sense, if you can understand the juxtaposition. For instance, cleaning up a budget irregularity caused by my previous boss which included: misappropriation of funds "borrowed" from other departments to allow an upgrade in our department's furnishings, all completed without proper authorization; Joe demanding that I terminate all supervisory subordinates who in his mind should have been aware of the financial irregularities to allow the upgrades; this directive to take action immediately "forthwith" if I can remember his statement correctly. In essence, there was no dialogue about policy and procedure protocol, just a "knee jerk" impulsive demand to correct a situation and management practice in the past that was long overdue, however done in a manner without thought of potential legalities being violated! That is, sense was "made" when it addressed maintaining power, aggression, ruthlessness, and degradation and used to promote his leadership! His unprofessional tone and conduct "took the cake" in nerve and guile, and I get a vote of NONCONFIDENCE from my supervisory staff!? But in their defense, they were not privy to what this man could become in his office domain. Hang on to your hats, we've just begun.

The night before my Thursday meeting, I thought long and hard about what might be its general theme. You just never knew with the administrator/director/autocrat—it depended on which voice and characterization of his personality was portrayed. I arrived at his office approximately five minutes early, quite frankly prepared for the worst. I summoned up my courage and knocked on the door.

"Come in, come in," he said. "Can I get you a coffee?"

Ah, the "normal" voice, I'm in luck, I thought. WRONG.

"I just want to say how much I appreciate your support throughout the past what, eighteen months. It has not gone unnoticed."

Damn, the "sexy" voice this time, move over Marilyn Monroe. I think I'm going to vomit! My response was short and to the point. "We are in a dreadful state of affairs and I'm wondering if we're on the same page administratively?" An extremely forthright statement to make to this particularly RUTHLESS personality! I felt in the "mind's eye" of what Hitler's generals must have felt when they confronted him during an operations meeting and were not just met with a rebuff, but open hostility and irrational rage!

In my situation, the administrator/director/autocrat's despotic side did not happen throughout most of the meeting. Not in the beginning nor middle portion of the meeting, and I quickly perceived he had few allies and needed support from anywhere and anyone. Perhaps the executive board had had enough. All of this ran through my mind by 2:07 p.m.

"I appreciate your frankness, and yes it has been a very difficult and perplexing arena to work in, hasn't it" was his response.

Ahha, maybe we're getting somewhere, the "normal" voice; maybe it's going to be a good meeting after all! WRONG. The choice of one particular word, *arena*, gave it away!!

For thirty minutes he talked and talked AND talked, and then stated abruptly, "I'm thinking of amalgamating two divisions into one, which will entail eliminating a director. I'm interviewing two directors. You happen to be one of them." Frankly, I was taken aback. From my viewpoint, a candidate for the director vacancy had to be very careful about the nature and quality of their response. It will be remembered in the future and possibly used against you in spades! I gave a direct response, because at that particular time I felt I had the upper hand; the worst he could do was ask for my resignation, which I was prepared to give!

My response was short and to the point. "Before I could take on such a role and the responsibilities incumbent in this new position I would want to see 'proof of practice'—in common English, a style of leadership coming from your office that is less formidable and more approachable for all involved."

After a pregnant pause Mr. Administrator/Director/Autocrat almost went across the desk at me!! The "admin" voice came through loud and clear. "WHO THE HELL D'YA THINK YOU'RE TALKING TO? YOU INSOLENT SACK OF SH . . . AND TO THINK WHAT I'VE DONE FOR YOU THE PAST EIGHTEEN MONTHS—I CARRIED YOU."

I sat quietly and felt in control for once during the past eighteen months. I felt truly in control—it was a wonderful, almost sensual feeling to respond in the following manner: "You're probably right in your comments about my lack of loyalty, but a forthright answer is better than a sniveling—" I was cut off and then some!

His response followed. "IF YOU THINK YOU'RE GOING TO PLAY JOHNNY ROCCO THE THIRD IN MY F . . . OFFICE YOU'VE GOT ANOTHER THINK COMIN' AND BY THE WAY I COULD HAVE YOUR LICENSE REVOKED."

I stood my ground. "That is your prerogative, but I'm wondering what statute in the code of conduct and practice standards of my profession have I contravened during the past twenty months, to be accurate? By the way, if I've contravened a practice standard I never received a challenge from you, the client constituency, or my peers. Be very careful how you proceed!" I purposefully left out the complaint from my immediate subordinates, the eight supervisors who had been shielded from the avalanche of bunk coming from this man's office.

This time, the administer/director/autocrat got up from his desk and very slowly, very methodically strode over to where I was sitting, walked behind me and started to speak, his head less than six inches from my left ear, rotating from side to side at the back of my head. "Malignant narcissist, does that ring a bell, Mr. Big Shot? Leading with impunity is like raping without conscience, shall I go on, Alpha Big Shot?"

In a microsecond I had processed what I'd feared the most during the past twenty months—that I'd been taped by a colleague, and this information passed on to Mr. administrator/director/autocrat or his collaborator, the controller (a personal friend from the past). I replied with integrity. "Yes, I stated those comments in a fit of frustration and rage." Inside I was SEETHING at my naïve, trusting stupidity; the comments had been taped and were now being used against me! They could be very easily transcribed, witnessed by a notary public, then sent to the registrar of my college, whose action could be anyone's guess, depending on how my defense or lack thereof was interpreted.

As I sat there, his body was still uncomfortably close, his head rotating back and forth beside then behind my head, as he talked several inches from my ear. The thought of the past twenty months flashed by in a microsecond, the "siege mentality" that we as a group of professionals had been put through! A snake pit of vampires and goblins was the way I'd described the organization to my friends, and I still stand by that statement!

The "admin" voice broke my concentration. "Your balls are in a vise, Mr. Big Shot, and there was never an option regarding your future in this organization, NEVER AN OPTION."

Before he could continue, I got up and said, in a matter-of-fact voice, "Do what you have to do, I'm through," and walked out the door.

In the background I heard him shout, "YOU'LL LEAVE WHEN I SAY YOU CAN LEAVE." I kept on walking.

I wrote a resignation letter and left it on my desk, gathered up my personal belongings, and had them boxed by the time the security police arrived to escort me from my office. Quite frankly, I was surprised by my behavior and exhilarated at the same time. No more tremor, fatigue, anger, frustration, condemning self-hatred!! No more marriage by convenience for him, hell on earth for me. It felt great! I was employed in a new job four months later; my former boss's modus operandi was by then well known in the professional community. Less than a year later, the executive board bowed to the myriad of complaints and voluminous evidence that indicted this man!! He was fired on Friday and given a severance package that would choke a horse, in my professional opinion. He went back to his old job, which he'd left five hundred miles away, THREE YEARS earlier!?? At the time I wondered how the hell he was allowed that extended period of time and still be able to return to his former job. How did that happen? What gives!? Reading one of my recent books would have provided the answer. By the way, nothing came of his threat regarding the college; he was too smart to risk a scandal this far along in the game and didn't want to risk losing a horse-choking severance package.

I invite you to complete the Psychopathy Spectrum Test for Joe: the administrator/director/autocrat. When you have completed the test, compare your results with the author's test results at the back of the book under the heading "Author's Test Results – Vignettes."

Vignette 4: Ned: "the Lead Pipe Cinch"

Ned "the lead pipe cinch" was aptly nicknamed due to his tendency to make extreme pronouncements when confronted about the obvious. For instance, wearing a yellow "slicker" raincoat in mid July, 85 degrees Fahrenheit weather during a heat wave, forecasted for two additional weeks. When confronted about his attire and fear of rain, his response was a rigid "my behavior is not your concern and the weather man is certainly not prophetic!". Ned was a professional rival who had been unceremoniously terminated *without cause* from his last job! He was a rival in the sense that he was competing for funding—which had been given to us at this brand-new agency I had just joined, and *not* to his former agency. Need I say more? And yes, he was the man who had passed me in the hall during the interview process prior to him being chosen as my agency's new CEO. He remembered me, and I certainly remembered him. We were two very competitive individuals; the chemistry wasn't there, and to say the least, I wasn't impressed with him—nor he with me, as it turned out!

This individual gave the first impression of having a clever mind (over time this was to be disputed). That is, he demonstrated speed and accuracy of integration, a quick interpretative processing ability—though still not as formidable as the administrator/director/autocrat's (see previous vignette). Overall, he was a very shrewd, conniving individual whose modus operandi was the "bottom line"—always the bottom line!

Let me reinforce what I'm talking about. We'd reviewed the vision and then mission/mandate of our new agency; this document had been developed by one of the most intelligent boards I'd had the privilege to work with during my (by now) ten-year career. In short, they had impressed me during the short period of time I was involved with them.

Then Ned "the lead pipe cinch" came out with one of his "pearls." "Jake, I don't really like what I'm reading, do you?"

My response—"How so?"—was not taken well.

"Jake, I'm not always right but I'm never wrong; I need dialogue, not conjecture." And with that, he walked away with a snort of indignation. Now, what the hell was that supposed to mean!?

Over the next several months a number of staff members were hired for the clinical program which I oversaw, in addition to several support staff. Of course, Ned "the lead pipe cinch" felt it necessary to demonstrate his authority on a regular basis, which inevitably, backfired over time. More specifically, people were left wondering, "Who the hell does this guy think he is"!? His ego, which was GIGANTIC, became a giant obstacle against developing a cohesive, loyal team of subordinates, to state it mildly. The comments by the staff were not kind.

"Why doesn't this guy zone into the '80s?"

"Is this guy for real? I thought servitude went out with segregation."

"What's his license plate number? I feel a road rage coming on."

Etcetera.

Unfortunately, Ned's ego was twice as lofty as his short stature and then some. He would often forgo the regular staff meetings in the boardroom and instead have the staff assemble in the hallway. What gives? His office, which incidentally was twice the size of mine and the other recently hired mid-manager's combined, was at the end of the hall. Over time approximately ten of us heeded the message and stood in the hallway outside our offices waiting for him to emerge from his office. He did so, DRAGGING A CHAIR behind him! He placed it in front of his door, proceeded to stand on it to give him additional height and from my perspective, lofty authority over the hoi polloi (underlings). You can imagine the reaction from the staff and the negative correlation between stated message and credibility; his purpose and intent became a silly spectacle and then some! This administrator of "great" intellectual vanity, slightly over five feet tall, stepping onto his chair then speaking to us about a subject that was as mundane as watching paint dry!

People tried to keep a straight face, bit their tongues, looked at the floor, looked at the ceiling, looked sideways. We were embarrassed, to put it mildly for him, not for us poor plebes.

After approximately fifteen minutes Ned "the lead pipe cinch" finished his soliloquy, stepped down from the chair, gave us a quick head nod, and re-entered his office, dragging the chair behind him then shutting the door. People re-entered their offices and then began the gales of laughter! People laughed so hard the security guard knocked on doors inquiring as to what the hell was going on. *Oh no, here we go again,* I said to myself, *a significant manifestation of management dysfunction with narcissism grossly interfering with insight/self-awareness.* Déja-vu flooded my brain, provoking the following question: *Am I going to play a "second banana" role and ONCE AGAIN be sucked into a self-defeating role I didn't want in the first place?! No,* I said to myself, *I'll sit back and let him self-destruct.* But it didn't happen, not on my watch anyway. I'm no hero, but pride—that silly g . . . damned word—entered the picture and bit me in the backside ONCE AGAIN.

Approximately one month later, as I attended a weekly staff meeting, I noticed an agenda item that puzzled me and subsequently enraged me! It read, "Standardized Annual Reviews." Nothing out of the ordinary, right? WRONG. If you can believe this, Ned "the lead pipe cinch" had attached the unabridged annual review of a colleague of mine *without* eliminating the identifying features—like his name!! You got it right, we were privy to my colleague's entire annual performance evaluation when he worked at Ned's former place of employment. I was dumbstruck and tried to articulate my vexation to Ned, whose response was equally unfathomable. "Jake, it's okay, calm down, he's moved to XYZ city." This city was two thousand miles away, but nevertheless! He then said, "I'm sure he wouldn't mind—we're all professionals here."

THE SILENCE IN THE ROOM WAS DEAFENING.

By the end of the week two more staff had submitted their resignations and left without notice. *Without notice* was almost unheard of in the mid-1980s, when there was still some semblance of loyalty and respect for companies. This entire scenario did *not* get back to the board executive and should have been an immediate priority, but it wasn't, and nothing happened! I suppose we naively hoped that Ned "the lead pipe cinch" would change or soften his behavior, or better still, leave on his own. At the time, and after the scandalous behavior mentioned above, a long-term working relationship with this man meant total abrogation of integrity. This was a "bottom line" guy!?? B.S. guy, you mean! "The end justifies the means" guy; "He who survives wins" guy; "Never say die, I'm going to win at all costs" guy!! You get the picture. I felt at this point, he would start making incessant demands on all of us individually that were TOTALLY unacceptable—and he did.

During the next several months, the staff found out that Ned "the lead pipe cinch" had a girlfriend accountant who co-owned a business with him, less than two blocks from our workplace. Ned "the lead pipe cinch" began spending increasingly more time at their business and increasingly less time at our agency. In a nutshell, it's called *conflict of interest* and *theft of time*! I won't bore you with the "goings on" over the next six months, but from the staff's perception there was immense fraud being perpetrated, blatant theft of time, which is unlawful and punishable by immediate termination and financial restitution in many cases! Individual board members were carefully selected by the staff and asked out to lunch, at which time Ned's behavior was described in detail. The respective board members could not believe someone would have the audacity, after approximately six months on the job, to work, at most, and I mean this without any exaggeration of understatement, TWO HOURS PER WEEK as an administrator of an agency! In conjunction, and also factored into their astonishment, Ned "the lead pipe cinch" had already come to our agency with a cloud over his head regarding the arbitrary downsizing of his former agency, which had a national reputation, and his subsequent termination *without cause* from his former employers! Why wouldn't that cause hesitancy/dissonance in taking action from a board member's perspective?! It should have been a giant red flag, but it wasn't; the story gets better! To answer the previous question, he must have had one hellova good interview to bipass board scrutiny, or good old fashioned luck!?

There was no union at our agency, which was too bad, because a Secret Staff Committee was finally formed of those of us who had ten years of experience or more and recognized a dramatic action plan needed to be developed and soon, or this new agency would internally combust.

During this period, Ned "the lead pipe cinch," in his infinite wisdom, decided to combine two units after deciding three "line" positions were redundant. Obviously, he felt the caseloads, which were already high, could be further expanded and dealt with competently by the remaining, albeit much-reduced staff complement. BAD MISTAKE; the agency's remaining staff were overwhelmed, which, by the way, marked the beginning of the end for Ned "the lead pipe cinch."

Eventually, after many more months, the Secret Staff Committee by this time had hired a "third party" investigator/ex police officer, who came back with enough evidence to put the kibosh on Ned "the lead pipe cinch." How so, you ask? There were over thirty photographs of him standing beside his girlfriend, taken at their place of business, two blocks away from our agency! Times and dates were placed underneath and stamped by a notary public. Unfortunately for Ned "the lead pipe cinch," they coincided with when he should have been working at our agency. The caper had worked; now the Secret Staff Committee set its next task to develop a cogent, "crisp" document that was not overstated, but demonstrated the extreme malfeasance that was being perpetrated! At one point during the investigation—and it is a laughable recollection—Ned "the lead pipe cinch" suggested to the board executive during a monthly meeting that they should hire his girlfriend to be the controller of the agency. "Of course, you know, she's a qualified accountant." The board almost took him up on it.

To finish off, you're probably wondering what ever happened to Ned "the lead pipe cinch." The board, in their infinite wisdom, incurred another six months of staff resignations, phone calls from beleaguered ex-staff waiting for their overdue records of employment, client complaints, and even a politician from the local riding threatening legal action! All of this before *real action* was taken—and not by the current board. The Secret Staff Committee requested a special board meeting which was granted "on camera" with a *new* board. They brought along the trusty document, entitled "In-House Longitudinal Study," which blew the socks off the *new* board executives, two of whom were university academics. From what I was told, the gales of laughter—actual howling by a number of board members at the magnitude of his preposterous behavior—could be heard on the streets below!

Two hours later, Ned "the lead pipe cinch" was tracked down by two executive board members at his place of business, and was informed, in front of his girlfriend, to, "Get your ass back to the agency, NOW." Ned "the lead pipe cinch" looked bewildered—at least according to the gossip mill—and of course his tendency to deny, rationalize, minimize things reared its ugly head for the last time—at our Agency anyway! He simply did *not* comprehend what was going on during the two-block walk back to the office! Both members of the board remained quiet in spite of his attempts to engage in conversation. I was told later on that Ned "the lead pipe cinch" thought it was some kind of deliberate sham to camouflage a surprise party, at which time the board executive would congratulate him for his brilliant leadership. Not quite; the board executive gave him a "tongue lashing" that would make a marine drill sergeant cringe. They vowed he would never, ever receive a reference, and in very short order, like two minutes or less, terminated him; this time he received "just cause." Two board members accompanied him to his office and gave him five minutes to collect his personal belongings, which he did, and then he left, never to work in the mental health industry again! At least, not in the last forty years of my career.

A pause for the cause before you begin the Psychopathy Spectrum Test. I digress for the moment to provide the following information. Most dysfunctional organizations operate from distorted thinking paradigms (models). Many of the problems occur when employees carry forward unresolved problems from outside of work (e.g., adult children of alcoholic parents) and use the organization milieu to work out their personal problems, agenda, and conflict on their colleagues! This damaging behavior creates chaos and havoc amongst the unwitting staff, with a negative effect on work productivity.

I invite you to complete the Psychopathy Spectrum Test for Ned "the lead pipe cinch." When you have completed the test, compare your results with the author's test results at the back of the book under the heading "Author's Test Results – Fifteen Vignettes."

Vignette 5: Nina: The Cretin "(Ex) Business Partner"

This professional, a mental health practitioner in her late forties, received immense deferential treatment from her colleagues, which I observed when I had an opportunity to share a table with her during a professional conference. Her book, published in the mid-1980s, vaulted her to international repute, supported by immense skill in her chosen profession which later on was identified as an immense contradiction. Very surprisingly, a few days after the conference, I got a phone call from Nina, wondering if I'd like to discuss a joint business venture/proprietorship providing evaluation/treatment/consultation in the mental health industry? Would I? It couldn't have happened at a better time, and honestly the potential income to be earned wasn't too shabby. However, I did worry—what if I couldn't meet her expectations, which were exceedingly high? She was a driven, Type A personality with an inquisitive mind, an IQ through the roof, and did not suffer fools gladly.

All of this drifted through my mind after the phone call, and despite some insecurity, I took the plunge. I returned her call the next day and stated, "Okay, then, let's get the ball rolling," and we did! Very quickly, we developed a business plan, identified both convergent and divergent job interests, and developed a vision and mission/mandate for the business. Cost benefits and cost effectiveness were also examined with investment optics in mind. All of which occurred over a nine-month period. Then, sliding along, we co-signed a five-year lease, moved into our joint offices, put our respective "shingles" on the door and—through my colleague's immense reputation—had an eight-month waiting list of clients in ten working days! Almost unheard of in those times and in the broad spectrum of clinical intervention both individual clientele and organizational milieus.

It seemed to be working like a charm, but somehow and I have to admit this, I felt like I was being "played" bit by bit over time, especially when her ex-husband stated, "Now I can live in peace, Jake—you can take over the babysitting role!" Kachunk, the antennae went up and when I approached my business associate, or more accurately by now my business partner, and disclosed her ex-husband's comment, her response was "Jake, Jake, he's jealous of my career and reputation—I can't really defend myself, can I?" In my head I agreed, but in my heart a danger signal went off! Why, oh why didn't I listen to those "spidy" feelings!? Famous last words, as they say.

So, the business was started, the clients began arriving in droves, and from a modest point of view, things were going A-OK, until the rental check bounced after our third month in operation! How in God's name could this happen? I questioned my colleague, and she came back with some gobbledygook response, which I bought hook, line, and sinker. You'd think I'd learn to listen to my heart as well as my head? I hadn't, it was her charm, that seductive, captivating charm, that reduced my defenses as I look back.

The manager of this very toney professional building came to us a few days later, "cap in hand," requesting the rent money. To digress, my colleague and I had arranged to pay each month's rent on the basis of percentage earned. Her income was 3:1 ratio of mine, therefore in theory, she paid a three times higher percentage of the monthly rent. In theory it sounds fair and above board, but in practice it caused immense problems! More specifically, I'd have to go each month and confront her—and even once or twice think seriously of going to small claims court—to get her share of the rent!

Another problem was a major hardship: I couldn't get out of this financial dilemma because we'd made the payment plan a legal arrangement. I was on the hook for the next five years of the lease.

There was no "escape clause" in the lease because the city we worked in had a thriving economy. Once you were in, you were stuck with the leasing conditions, which were draconian (severe) to say the least, or I could find someone else to take over the contracted leasing arrangements, but my partner's reputation, by this time, reduced this possibility substantially! More specifically:

I eventually learned that NO ONE, BUT NO ONE historically, who dealt with my business partner, walked away unscathed! It just so happened that I was no exception. I could not, throughout four of the five years I worked with her, find anyone to take over the lease! Although I advertised regularly, no one in the industry was foolhardy enough to come and join forces with my colleague! They were happy to send referrals, but did not want to get involved in any potential "rumbles" with this individual; it appears everybody knew her better than Jake!

But I forgot to finish my story with the building manager demanding our monthly rent. I had to use my Visa card for that particular month's rent. Although I was promised by my colleague that she'd pay me back, it never happened!

After that, approximately six months of our rental payment arrangement went along smoothly. I got the feeling that things were finally going to work out and in fact be quite successful. Then the rent check bounced ONCE AGAIN and was returned NSF. I'm not ashamed to say I went to this cretin eleven times to get her share of the rent, which never happened. The building manager was breathing down our necks after three weeks of overdue rental payment—wouldn't you?! ONCE AGAIN I had to pull out my trusty Visa card to pay this month's overdue rent! And ONCE AGAIN didn't get repaid!!

A few months later I made the mistake of going out for a lunch with my business partner. At that point, I found out where the money was really going! The woman had an impulse control disorder and was, in lay terminology . . . a SHOPAHOLIC! Our lunch cost me in excess of one hundred dollars—a lot more money in the mid-1990s than now—and Jake was about to witness her problem first hand!

While strolling along a major street of this Midwestern city, she stopped dead in her tracks. "I just have to have that," she said, after spying a jacket in a clothing store. She walked in, tried on an "all weather" coat, and then had the tailor make a few adjustments. She had just made a $1300 impulse purchase—in the space of twenty minutes! And that's nothing—three months later, after complaining about the two-year-old "piece of shit" she was driving (her words, not mine), she went car shopping with her Platinum American Express Card. This happened, once again, after conveniently forgetting to pay her share of the rent at our very toney office for the THIRD TIME!! This time according to her debriefing which always included snippets of the truth interspersed with exagerated inventions. She entered an Asian car dealership and asked to see two or three sports cars she had observed in the show room while driving by in her "piece of shit." She was shown the cars, chose the brightest-colored one and in her words, took it for a scenic drive at speeds IN EXCESS of one hundred miles per hour. You might call it an excursion into hell, just to get a feel for its "power, guts, and performance" as she stated nonchalantly-whatever turns you on!

When they returned to the dealership, she asked the salesperson when the car could be ready for her. He smiled and said, "On Thursday," which was two days hence. Her response, "I need to have it by the end of today, or you've lost a sale." This caused nary a pause by the salesperson, who responded, "No problem, we'll have it ready by four p.m." This scenario sums up the level, or better stated, the degree of pathological impulse spending my colleague was capable of committing! Unbelievable but true, and to reiterate, she used her PLATINUM AMERICAN EXPRESS CARD TO PURCHASE THIS VERY EXPENSIVE SPORTS CAR. One of seven credit cards she possessed. I know because she bragged about them and then showed them to me later on. Her rationale for overspending using credit cards instead of cash, was that it was "magic money," which caused me to shudder at the time. Let's continue.

One winter weekend she disclosed the following tale to me. After completing back-to-back reports, at which time my business partner stated she was up probably twenty-four hours, using a coffee addiction to keep her awake. She decided a "breather" for a few days skiing in the mountains was just what the doctor ordered. Subsequently, she further disclosed that while driving to the mountains in her brand-new sports car, fell asleep at the wheel at approximately six p.m. (darkness falls early in the Midwest). She went off the road and traveled approximately fifty yards through a snowy field by the side of the highway. That's traveling at an accelerated speed and then some!

She woke up around midnight, didn't know where she was or what had happened, and tried to get out of the car, which was, of course, buried in the snow. After approximately half an hour of struggling to open the door jammed against the snow, she made enough room to squeeze out of the vehicle. At this point, in pitch darkness mind you, she retraced her steps by walking along the tread line back to the highway. She then "thumbed" a ride to a nearby ski resort and hired a tow truck at a twenty-four-hour truck stand. UNBELIEVABLE, but true! According to her story, she told the tow truck driver some "cock and bull" story about her brakes giving out in order to elicit sympathy and got the sympathy vote big-time. I heard his decision was duly influenced when she leaned over and gave him an eyeful of cleavage with those C-cup bosoms. A joke was spread throughout the building where we worked, that after this escapade she received a greatly reduced towing rate, one starts to wonder, doesn't one!

Approximately one month later, she invited a mutual colleague to go skiing with her in the USA. The problem was (as always) my cretin business partner's gigantic ego interfered with reality, concerning her ability to ski. She had always stated she was a "black diamond" skier, meaning she could handle the most challenging hills. This was complete nonsense, which nearly cost her her life! Unfortunately, our mutual colleague had taken her comments at face value, believing my business partner's ability to ski at an expert level!

Towards the end of the day, they took the gondola up to the top of this incredibly high, very steep mountain. At this point, our mutual colleague skied halfway down the hill, occasionally looking over her shoulder for our heroine—who never arrived at the bottom! After waiting patiently for fifteen minutes, at which time it was starting to get dark our mutual colleague was getting worried! She decided to complete one last ski run and then contact the ski patrol if my business colleague was nowhere to be seen. When our mutual colleague got to the bottom of the hill beside the ski chalet, there, on a big "white board" was a message stating our heroine's name and the HOSPITAL where she could be reached.

You can imagine the response from our mutual colleague! She RAN into the ski chalet, explained who she was, and got on the telephone pronto. Our heroine, according to the ward nurse, had sustained a mild concussion and broken left clavicle, but would be okay to chat, and wanted visitors desperately! It goes without saying: this was a costly weekend, both emotionally and financially for our mutual colleague! One major issue before I forget! Our concussed heroine according to our mutual colleague had MISPLACED HER PURSE and couldn't pay one cent of that very extravagant impulse for a weekend respite from work. Who paid, you wonder? Our mutual, soon-to-be ex-colleague, now our mutual benefactor, soon-to-be mutual enemy, that's who!

Eventually she was paid back, but only after a lawyer was retained. I know because I saw the "Letter of Warning" and then the "Letter of Intent"—and it was a doozy! On to the next vignette, which is a continuation of this one, just for a change of protocol.

Vignette 6: Nina: The Cretin Cont'd

Two years later, YES, I lasted that long working with this devious, cold-blooded individual! We met with her very expensive and very competent chartered accountant! He "blew my socks off" when he stated in a forthright manner that my colleague's "depleted resources were a direct consequence of her excessive impulsive spending habits." No kidding, Ace! Shortly thereafter, I tried sitting down for a heart-to-heart conversation with my cretin business partner, who, by this time, I DESPISED. The following I say with the utmost contempt, the lady with the international, grade A, gold standard, professional reputation, my infected foot!? The attempted heart-to-heart was the WRONG approach. She laughed me off like second-hand news, told me it was "all in my head," and that I was "conspiring against her" along with her very expensive and competent chartered accountant. Oh dear!

I started to ruminate about my current situation, my future, and the drawbacks of working with this cretin, whose behavior was destabilizing my marriage. I was told I was an enabler and if I stayed in the current business arrangement, I deserved everything she dished out! People questioned my personal code of conduct and the ethics of staying in a business arrangement, or any arrangement with this revolting person. Even her ex-spouse, in so many words, stated, "I told you so (stupid)."

Then it happened—and I was there! My business partner's very expensive and competent chartered accountant was contacted by the Federal Government income tax collection agency! This happened because he had taken over as the executor of my business partner's finances—you guessed it, because she was hopelessly in debt. He was told in no uncertain terms that a check for $10,000 was expected, which unbeknownst to him had been promised by my business partner to be paid three days hence, "as a show of good faith." He phoned me to inquire if I knew anything about this arrangement, and by the way, he was TAPING the conversation! *Oh great, what did I get myself into!* I answered the accountant's questions very thoroughly, as I had nothing to hide. He then stated, "I think it best we have a tête-à-tête with our colleague sooner rather than later!" I agreed, and after a number of unanswered phone calls, written messages, and circuitous corridor encounters (she feigning time constraints), a meeting was eventually arranged, at which time my cretin colleague attempted to blame everyone else for her financial woes !? Are you surprised?

The meeting became a battle ground of wits, ostensibly a fight between the chartered accountant, a highly intellectual and very experienced professional, who was challenging the veracity of another highly intelligent professional, with an international reputation AND who was very slick! How slick was she, you ask? The full extent of this woman's devious cunning came out during that fateful meeting. More specifically, the frightening impact of her manipulative ploys to discredit and redirect any responsibility for her current financial nightmare was projected onto other people. This was a cold-blooded, sinister individual, no qualms in denigrating, maligning, misrepresenting, and bold-face lying to avoid responsibility for her devious actions! Her brilliant mind had never, ever been better. I had seen her work magic in the courtroom as an expert witness regarding mental health issues, winning many complex cases for the legal firms who hired her, but her eloquence, or better stated, grandiloquence (pompous eloquence) that day topped them all!

The chartered accountant recognized he had hit a stone wall regarding my cretin business partner's denial and rationalization of any responsibility for her financial dilemma. OUR financial dilemma, to be more accurate, as I was tied in legally by co-signing the lease and being a business colleague for a long duration, therefore viewed by most sources as "complicit in her deviant behavior." Nice position to be in, right?! The chartered accountant began by asking my business partner what had made her return to Great Britain ten years previously. I became dumbfounded but sat quietly, absorbing the interplay between these two verbal titans, syllable by syllable, phrase by phrase. After verbal swordplay of approximately ten minutes my business partner finally disclosed that a property she co-owned with her by now ex-husband, in another part of the country, had been seized to pay "back taxes." She blamed her ex-husband's financial incompetence, which might have been true, but now the chartered accountant's ploy identified the sinister depth of cold-blooded deceit we were dealing with!

The question was repeated by the chartered accountant, why had she and her ex-husband *at that specific time* decided to leave the country ten years previously?! She postured, hummed and hawed, and then said nothing! The final answer, which was the true answer, was unceremoniously shoved in front of her! Here it comes!

A letter from the Federal Government income tax department, fifteen years old and almost yellow with age, stated eight years of back taxes was owed, and their home was being expropriated in order to retrieve taxable income. I wondered how much was not stated!? Obviously, there was still a great deal more tax that was owed AND the Federal Government is persistent when investigating such blatant irregularities, and over time gets its man or woman in this case! You guessed it—once again my colleague blamed her ex-husband's ineptness and sat there wondering what would be her next move! It was her "proof" against our "proof" in the verbal interplay that unfolded.

The chartered accountant then proceeded in a carefully staged, modulated voice to describe, again with copies of letters from the income tax department, "requests" to pay the remaining back taxes. But by that time my colleague and her ex-husband had fled and were in another country. In that era (1980s) it was difficult to deport. someone regarding tax issues, especially if they were incognito (i.e., difficult to find).

The chartered accountant then produced "warning" letters from the income tax people to respond to the request to pay the remaining back taxes. Lastly, a final warning letter was produced, stating the back taxes were still owed and collecting compound interest, meaning interest on interest was accruing at an exponential rate day by day, and how was this going to be paid!?

ONCE AGAIN, my former business colleague sat there nonchalantly, blaming her ex-spouse and his incompetence in managing their finances. Further letters from the income tax department warned that returning to this country would initiate prosecution by the government, if the back taxes owed were not paid forthwith!! By the couple's lack of response, it appeared they had *no* intention of ever returning! Oh yeah?!

To digress, I had been approached earlier by a colleague in our office building to take over the duration of the lease (approximately eighteen months) because he was expanding his business, and was aware of my lease arrangement (and my colleague's abandonment) and wanted to remain at this location. *There is a God*, I thought, and signed the co-leasing arrangement post haste. Questions were asked about you-know-who, my responses were my responses, let's leave it at that.

Back to the story, after two years of being abroad, the dubious pair had returned to this country, much to the delight of the income tax collection department I'm sure. Why return, you ask? It appears the couple could *not* sustain a lifestyle in Great Britain to which they were accustomed! They had returned to "face the music" because they no longer had borrowing capabilities, due to their horrendous credit rating!

Once again, during the subsequent court proceedings, by this time in the mid-1990s, my cretin ex-business partner sat there impassively and began to YAWN!? I had been invited as a witness for the prosecution and was delighted to be there to tell my side of the story. But unfortunately I was not called to provide testimony, for reasons unknown, I can only surmise they felt my testimony was not required at this point in the trial, which in my humble opinion would have provided damning evidence! Moving on, the chartered accountant, who had forensic training, told me he had seen the cretin's type of "frozen" behavior throughout his career as an expert forensic authority. That is, the denial/rationalization, minimization "stagnant" facial expression. Or, as he described it, " white-collar scammers ruminate a game plan on the fly; what you're observing is intense concentration while they run through options. It's like playing a chess match with themselves." The chartered accountant had a lot to lose if he lost the case. I believed rightly or wrongly that he was testifying as a "hostile witness" under government threat of collusion to defraud, if he refused. Remember, he had been her accountant for many years. The following cross-examination was brilliant and captivating in its thoroughness and condemnation of what the miscreant had conspired to achieve to escape prosecution and defend her actions by blaming others, including her ex- husband.

The chartered accountant then proceeded to read an itemized transcript of the couple's deplorable conduct ten years prior, when they were frequently requested to pay their income tax debt. The presentation started with describing that fateful day when the collection agents interrogated this dubious pair—who had accumulated $778,000 in back taxes, multiply this by 5:1 ratio to bring it to a 2024 equivalence of $3.890,000,000. Remember, this trial was in the mid-1990s.

To make a long story short, a judgment was made *not* to incarcerate the couple!? I believe this happened because their combined income while working allowed dividing the taxable amount into equal shares owed by each spouse to be paid off in a reasonable period of time. WHICH WAS A GENEROUS DISPOSITION by the court, in my opinion. If the pair worked hard and lived on a conservative allowance, the debt could be paid off in five to seven years, or so I calculated.

Moving forward five plus years post trial, I learned from sources that it appeared the former spouse was well on the road to paying off his share of the debt. However, my ex-business partner cretin had *not* touched her debt owed, which was growing exponentially, every hour of the day, every day of the year! The laugh, and it was a big one, occurred in one of the stenographer "bullets" from court during the fateful trial just mentioned. It described my colleague's misunderstanding of the original meeting with collection services when they returned from overseas. The pair thought the meeting with the collection agents was a return home "welcome wagon"??! In essence, a coffee klatch to discuss the "frivolous income tax problem." As the chartered accountant read on, the report further detailed my ex-colleague's casual reaction to this unbelievable amount of money owed (for that period) as an "obvious error" by the government AND a complete misunderstanding of the motive for my colleague and her former husband accomplice's departure to their original homeland!? In addition, the report described her exaggerated *lack* of comprehension that leaving this country and moving to their country of origin would *not* have a repatriation consequence. AS IN *POTENTIAL PROSECUTION* if she did not pay their back taxes forthwith! The report also stated that the income tax agents had cautioned my ex-business partner numerous times about this attempted deceit. They felt it was highly unlikely, with her level of intelligence, educational accomplishments, and international reputation, that she did not understand the consequences of income tax evasion. After this devastating indictment, I re-iterate, the couple did *not* receive jail time.

You're probably wondering what ever happened to my cretin ex-business partner. As I recall, almost seven years later (early 2000s) a colleague from the city where our business had been located, sent me an e-mail suggesting I look at the paper's business section, which he had scanned. THERE IT WAS—BOLD AS LIFE!! My cretin ex-business partner had been "defrocked" from her professional association and sued for the expenses incurred during a legal battle, which she failed to win. She was also sued by various clients who had been collateral damage over the years of involvement with her, which I'm sure was identified as emotional abuse! I include my former business partner's favorite expression, "collateral damage," which she often used to rationalize her dirty dealings with angry, disconsolate victims—me included!

One last point: my former colleague was currently incommunicado, nowhere to be found!

I invite you to complete the Psychopathy Spectrum Test for the Cretin: ex business partner. When you have completed the test, compare your results with the author's test results at the back of the book under the heading "Author's Test Results – Fifteen Vignettes."

Vignette 7: Casey: The Second-in-Command

In the late 1980s, I purposely demoted myself to a mid-management position supervising about forty staff within twelve disciplines. Three weeks earlier, I'd sat down in the boardroom of a major hospital facility somewhere in North America, giving what I still maintain is the best interview of my career! Lo and behold, I got the job and started almost immediately. I was still only thirty-seven years old but a "shop worn" thirty-seven! The budget was okay, my boss, the executive director, was a right-wing bureaucrat who played favorites like nobody's business. During the interview, and of major concern, was her evident fear of her immediate subordinate. As it turned out, another ruthless predator! This second-in-command person loved, no she bathed, in power and control, was a master of the double entendre, the "cut and thrust" of senior management repartee! Over time, I learned to admire her ability to wield this ruthless authority with little, if any, fear of retribution—people were truly intimidated by her coercive power!! No one during the four years I was her subordinate *directly* challenged her behavior. NO ONE.

At our first meeting, she addressed me formally by last name, asking me twice to remind her what my first name was, which she immediately forgot. She set down the modus operandi of her supervision expectations, which was as follows: Her two cohorts, not as bright as she and metaphorically speaking two thugs really, would visit every Friday afternoon from one until two p.m. I was to present them with a pre-arranged document detailing and itemizing my staffing strengths and needs, budgetary updates, short- and long-term goal achievements vis-à-vis the mission mandate and optics of the organization. At the time, I felt this was not irregular. How wrong was I!

Over time a ripple effect occurred throughout the organization, ostensibly mimicking the idiosyncratic management practices of the second-in-command, not copying her practices exactly, but utilizing her draconian methods to ensure "consistency, efficiency and effectiveness." These were her three favorite words, which I heard repeatedly throughout my four-year tenure under her reign of terror! Let me provide some examples.

A colleague with an equivalent-sized program to mine ran staff meetings like a drill sergeant. During weekly case conferences, he demanded that each representative—which numbered about a dozen—utilize the same presentation format. That is, the same headings and areas to be covered, describing specific sets and subsets to be monitored. It sounds practical but wasn't workable for a variety of reasons, and to be blunt, too many to discuss at this time. Subsequently, the ANXIETY—rigid, anticipatory anxiety—exhibited by this insecure manager, was high and easily fueled to ignition—if the various disciplines did *not* adhere exactly to his directives!

This contre-coup, "ricochet" effect tempted fate big time, in reprimands and outbursts from my colleague. I guess you could call it osmosis, as he began to reflect the second-in-command's neurotic exactness and "standard of excellence," her words again. Superficially this authoritarian, command style of management bastardized a Total

Quality Management approach by attempting to copy its tenets of: quality control, quality improvement, internal and external customer satisfaction. Unfortunately, the ingredients of this management style were horribly demeaned, which caused rigidity and reactivity amongst the staff, the antithesis of Total Quality Management's potential creativity! In English, the format was stifling, and promoted animosity, staff dissension, and militant opposition to change. The "blinkers" were on and stayed on for a very long period of time because of the rigidity of this bastardized management style.

Another example was a "Centralized Referral System," which was put in place by the second-in-command "to combat duplication and wastage of staff time." Specifically, a triage team was developed to manage and vet the referrals coming into the center. On paper it sounded good. The team would match the referrals and level of estimated care and attention the clientele required with an appropriate clinical program/unit. Here is the problem! The managers of the respective programs in this "Centralized Referral System" became quickly aware of favoritism, regarding easier case referrals going to the friends of the triage team. If you were on the "outs" with this team, you got stuck with the more difficult and demanding referrals! The obvious result: increased "burnout" rate, which was much higher on a per capita basis on a team which was "on the outs."

Those therapeutic teams "on the outs" consistently obtained patient referrals needing moderate to high care requirements! Forget about the criteria that was set up for referrals to be dispersed *appropriately*— which, by the way, had taken upwards of a year to develop and standardize. Yes, the second-in-command had developed on paper a very "consistent, efficient, and effective" intake process! But in practice, it was bastardized and undermined by in-fighting politics and all the other adjectives that have a pejorative (negative) meaning. The managers of the care units met once per week, Monday mornings from nine to eleven, fifteen managers representing twelve different disciplines. This meeting was chaired by the second-in-command, with a slapdash "cut and thrust" scathing vitriol that was actually quite pristine IN ITS CRUELTY. Think of the actress Glenn Close playing a refined Don

Rickles, sprinkled with Bob Newhart mannerisms/quips and you've got an idea of what transpired in those weekly, two-hour diatribes! No one, but no one, could match her acerbic nature during the meeting, but afterwards was another story, as her behavior influenced some of the more insecure managers to try copying her style. Unbelievable but true, and who got it in the end? You guessed it, the "grunts," who else, the front-line workers that did all the basic case work!

Over time, the line staff wondered what the hell had gone wrong this week, which repeated itself each week ad infinitum. Inevitably, there was always some kind of newfangled, "revised" system developed and brought forward to try out on the units and the grunts within the units. The mounting discord by the staff set in motion an emotional continuum, ranging from the doldrums to dysphoric (depressive) haze! A steady supply of "technique," for lack of a better word, was manufactured to "improve working conditions on the units." It was thought up and packaged by senior management, BUT originated from, guess who, the second-in-command, and to my knowledge, was never thoroughly discussed prior to implementation with the mid managers. What gives here?! They became scapegoated by the poor grunts who had to operationalize each mundane revision (or else)! All of this change encouraged siege mentality by the staff; grunts versus junior mid management, "pistols at dawn" scenarios.

The rationale for all these changes was to promote staff morale. HAH! Practice "trials" were developed using various techniques, which typically failed. Why, you ask? The animosity stated above reared its ugly head is the answer! Staff would undermine junior management, which included me, and over time we turned a blind eye." Obviously, this passive aggressive behavior was not good to say the least. Passive aggression is not me, by the way. However, and to reiterate our predicament: Over time we had become too overwhelmed to bother attempting to change things, or in fact take staff to task when confronted with insubordinate and increasingly negligent behavior. We, the mid management, were disconsolate, having limited energy to challenge the grunt's inappropriate behavior and attempt to make change occur. Nope, we were a beaten group, emotionally exhausted, and the last thing we wanted was to complete additional work. We were too depleted to follow through, above and beyond a regular day's workload!

Thinking back to those times as I dictate this book still brings forward suppressed memories of how vicious "wolf pack" mentality can become.

That's when the staff decided to form a Secret Committee to address the situation.

Here we go again! The members of the Secret Committee had had enough and developed a detailed action plan to collect data that would support an indictment against administration, which would then be submitted to the board of directors overseeing the senior management.

To make a long story short, the data started rolling in and the results were very promising, more specifically, the second-in-command was NOT making the grade! The behavioral dimensions of attitude being assessed by the Secret Committee were indicating a negative valence (transfer) "across the board" for this woman's intake system to improve "consistency, efficiency, effectiveness"!! The brilliant idea to compare each of five attitude factors, with an absolute standard of expected management practice also did the trick! After approximately six months of investigation, an indictment of her behavior was to be submitted to external forensic evaluators! Again, that was the plan.

This indictment assessing the allegations of the second-in-command's failure to manage appropriately, in fact, in a great many areas, reflected her markedly inferior work performance "spinning the tires," wasting money, essentially desecrating staff morale. Now, what to do with the data collected?

It was decided a representative from the Secret Committee would take the information while masking the identity of the second-in-command, and meet with a local politician with ties to the funding body of the organization. At which time, they would complete a presentation of the data, in a report entitled "Effectiveness Evaluation of Management Protocol." At the end of the presentation, which described basic indictments of senior management behavior overseeing the organization, the politician's response we envisioned might be, "I would love to know who this phantom Manager is, but I understand you can't breach confidentiality." The basic supposition being, a crafty politician could see "feathering their bed" politically by addressing this situation quickly and then reaping the political benefits from the subsequent scandal.

If there was a potential for scandal, which in this case was inevitable, they would want to proceed post haste, and that is exactly what happened! The politician organized, within three weeks, an external body of forensic examiners to investigate the management protocol, its style, format, and impact on the organization and its ultimate downfall.

The "Effectiveness Evaluation of Management Protocol" report was brought forward with the identity of the manager masked but used as Exhibit A on how NOT to run an organization. The forensic team submitted its fateful decision. If it hadn't been for the second-in-command's seventeen-year tenure, she would have lost her job the very next day! The examiners' findings indicated gross negligence which should have resulted in immediate expulsion of the senior management team! This recommendation came from a thorough forensic evaluation of the overall administrative practices of the organization.

Justice had finally prevailed—or so we thought! Nope, unfortunately the scapegoat was the second-in-command's cowardly superior, who "got the axe." But that's the way it goes in senior management. Here today, gone tomorrow in many situations! The second-in-command was given a lateral transfer to a much smaller portfolio, a big slap in the face for that cruel, demeaning woman, poetic justice be damned! Why the bitter tone, Jake?

I remember the wake of talent that was lost because of the second-in-command's egregious behavior over the years. Unfortunately, nothing was done until the staff, for the sake of survival, took matters into their own hands. Once again, this was a non-union shop.

I invite you to complete the Psychopathy Spectrum Test for Casey: the second-in-command. When you have completed the test, compare your results with the author's test results at the back of the book under the heading "Author's Test Results – Fifteen Vignettes."

Vignette 8: George: The Executive Director

It was the fall of 1976. I was living in a small city and had competed successfully for a position at a national organization with many branches throughout the country. The basic job duties entailed running seven programs throughout the week for children and young adolescents. A nice "gig" as they say, or so I thought, until my "honeymoon period" was over. George the Executive Director had a major problem with social propriety. Let me go on; this will be a short vignette as I remained at this particular job exactly six months (which felt like six years).

George the Executive Director was a chain smoking, obese man in his early forties who looked and acted ten years older. He was, to put it mildly, a workaholic; he ate, slept and ruminated about his job duties, AND before I forget, did a lot of "shmoozing" with the higher ups! That was his forté. He was smart with budgeting but a micro manager, and, to be frank, his understanding of organizational dynamics was "bent" in a sadistic kind of way. As I found out very quickly. "When you work for me, it's my way or the highway, now leave, I'M BUSY" was his attitude! A notable thing I observed after a few weeks of employment was his shallow, phony persona. His attitude toward the staff was very, very abrupt when he was under pressure, and he NEVER EVER suffered fools gladly. More about that one—he could dish it out but could not take it! To his wife, which was frequently observed on a daily basis by the writer and his colleagues, George was brittle, argumentative, and sarcastic with a giant S. To his five-year-old little boy, a beautiful kid, he was authoritarian, very exacting in his expectations of behavior and very, very blunt with a tone of rejection, often stating, "I'm busy, NOT NOW" when interrupted by this very lonely boy.

Conversely, around senior executive personnel, as the saying goes, butter wouldn't melt in George's mouth. During the encounters, I observed that his suave, calming, "let me help you" ploy was honed to a "T." The senior management generally liked and respected him. Which thankfully changed significantly over time!

After three months, my immediate boss the second-in-command, a young woman approximately my age, submitted a very short notice of termination (less than two weeks), abandoning her job, in basic English. As well, she left her husband of three years who was dumbfounded, until he found out she had been having an affair with her tennis partner. On the day she left (she had not yet informed the staff) we noticed her having a meeting with George the Executive Director in his office and could overhear his loud, abrasive tone through the door, which he always kept slightly ajar. This technique, we presumed was to let everyone know that HE WAS THE BOSS. It worked—being ordered into his office was not fun; before the meeting, during the meeting, and after the meeting, when you were licking your wounds. He made sure that no one but he won those famous battles!

The meeting between them was brief, and then my immediate boss walked out to the general office area with George close behind, who, with finger pointed, motioned her to stand beside him. What followed was startling. He began with a general harangue of the woman, starting with "I feel like I've been stabbed in the back fifty times! I don't really condone 'quick how-are-yas and then quick see-ya-later stunts! Use this as an example of what I WILL NOT TOLERATE IN THE FUTURE!!" And with that grandiose, underhanded, threatening speech, he left the young woman in shock and starting to cry!! Welcome to my world for the next several months, although at that time it felt like three condemning decades! The abuse didn't end with her departure.

The young woman's replacement and now second-in-command, was what my colleague and I surmised was a high functioning adult with autism. Let me provide a snapshot picture of Sandra: socially inept, but in some respects a highly intelligent woman. Her interpersonal deportment lacked warmth and was very focused and linear, with limited ability to think "outside of the box." She was reticent to disclose anything about her past job experiences/responsibilities, nor did she show interest in her colleagues' backgrounds. We identified this behavior as "ghosting people" before they had an opportunity to form an opinion, let alone a professional relationship! Simply put, exceedingly limited personal information was provided by her throughout my tenure at this job. How in the world did George find this VERY remote, mono-dimensional automaton to oversee staff, let alone deal with the occasional complaint call from an irate client!? When this occurred, she was blunt and frequently dismissive unless it was a board member or a board executive. She was astute enough to know which side her bread was buttered on!

Over the ensuing weeks we, as a small group of five staff, found her insecurities projected onto our quality of work and with each staff, an overriding feeling that their work performance was going to be denigrated. In fact, some people were harassed on a daily basis. This new second-in-command was "obsessed with accuracy" (her expression) and with limited to zero interpersonal skills, could be incredibly demeaning in her blunt, critical tone and subsequent belittling comments. By now you probably recognized her behavior mimicked George the Executive Director! You got it right! She frequently complimented his ability to focus on problems until in her words, "they were resolved regardless of the time and consequence," which were his famous words. Yes, that was her statement as well throughout my tenure at the job. Basically, in her mind if the problem was solved by George, it was solved regardless of the consequences, which in the future became his downfall!

It never ended that the subordinate workers were required to stay way over their prescribed work time (this was another non-union shop). That was an expectation from George the Executive Director, and he frequently approached staff at the last moment on many occasions to complete extra duty. To many it became very apparent this abuse of authority reduced his personal anxiety but reinforced his tendency to be obsessive. If the individual didn't oblige his request, the next week was hell for that person! That is, listening ad nauseum to snide comments, undermining hostile innuendos, all of which is currently labelled *harassment*. Fifty years ago, it was called "taking shit from the boss"! Guess who copied this vitriol in spades? My immediate boss Sandra, the second-in-command, Ms. Savage Imitator (S.I) for short. Frequently S.I would quietly walk behind a staff member and look over their shoulder; several times I would hear a squeak to a minor scream as the staff member felt S.I's breath on their neck. A complaint would often mean attending a three-way conference with the complainant, George the Executive Director and S.I., in George's office, door slightly ajar! Not fun, believe me, I had one of those meetings. I describe it in the next paragraph.

Several months later I was sent (I had no choice) to a large national convention in a very upscale neighborhood in Toronto several hundred miles away. Why me? Who knows, but I suspected it was a political device by George to embellish himself (once again) with his superiors. I drove to the conference and arrived on time but found I was the only representative from a small(ish) community office and therefore received more than my share of silly questions.

"Do you ride on horseback or in your car to work?"

"Your slang is a bit outdated, we don't talk like that here."

"I dig your outfit, but not your aftershave" was my mocking retort.

I quickly realized why I was chosen. George would have put somebody through the wall if they talked to him like that. Nonetheless, I gave as well as I received and ended up being approached by several staff suggesting I transfer to their locale if I had the chance.

One of the events during the initial stages of the conference was attending "ice breaker" meetings (not one but several). In one of these meetings, we were asked to construct a clay design and discuss its theme, that was fun and creative; no one said anything untoward about the one I designed, and I was proud to take it with me to show the staff back at work. A BIG MISTAKE.

When I returned to the office, I showed the clay design to several staff who were curious about the conference and the ice breaking techniques we had used, emphasizing personal creativity, etcetera. The comments were positive until S.I arrived late for work, and in a MOOD. She verbally tore the clay design to pieces and stated she would bring this ISSUE to the attention of George the Executive Director. When George arrived—you guessed it—I was invited to his office for a "three-way"—no pun intended. Over the next thirty minutes, I was accused of purposefully ruining HIS organization, HIS reputation, and HIS subordinates' reputation! Unfortunately, all of this nonsense was reinforced by me not providing a rebuttal, as by this time, I had had enough! George's behavior, enmeshed with Sandra, his second-in-command's "puppy dog" mimicking had exhausted my stamina. I had to resign.

Oh yes, one last slap in the face: he purposely refused (or purposely forgot) to provide my travel expenses! I thought about civil action, but it would not have accomplished anything on account of the extended back-up in the court system. Instead, I had the TENACITY, his word not mine, to return and demand the travel expenses, which he slowly pulled from his drawer, stating he forgot about it at the time. His final parting words stung: "The lack of work from you the past six months should be enough to never, ever get you another job in this industry. I have contacts, you know!" He handed me the check and said, "THERE'S THE DOOR," nodding for me to leave. Which I did, and not too soon, I might add!

Many years later, I received the following information which quite frankly did *not* surprise me! George's five-year-old son was apprehended by the Children's Aid Society and placed in care; George had an acrimonious divorce with his wife; George was terminated by the national council of his organization for embezzlement, which had begun in 1974, according to forensic auditors; the building structure where we worked was ordered demolished, and the organization's status within the parent body was found in gross dereliction of its duties and stricken from the national agency list! Last but not least, George was fired and died of a heart attack a few years later.

I invite you to complete the Psychopathy Spectrum Test for George: the Executive Director. When you have completed the test, compare your results with the author's test results at the back of the book under the heading "Author's Test Results – Fifteen Vignettes."

Vignette 9: Gazlen

Not so long ago, I was at a point in my career where I had begun to think about retirement from the nine-to-five grind. I would still be open to the occasional consultation contract, but casework, when you're in your late sixties, starts to lose its attraction. A new member of the staff joined, an older man of slightly younger years than I, who had a positive reputation, or so we thought.

Here is the problem: this individual had run his own business after qualifying later in life and gained a positive reputation through hard work at two separate business offices in two communities. In my mind, and my colleagues' minds, we thought he would be a marked asset to the organization. Thinking back as I write this vignette, this person was at first hesitant to open up with personal disclosures. *No problem*, I thought, *he's obviously no fool*. I had learned through personal experience that too much transparency during the "honeymoon period" of a job can cost you big time. How so? There are individuals looking to feed off your kindness, and upon reflection it seems they view this trait as a weakness in character. More specifically, they interpret kind and congenial behavior as an insecurity, a person that avoids conflict and confrontation, and thus easy prey for the predator. The following is a systematic description of how we were "played" by the man I call Gazlen over a period of two years, give or take a few months.

Within three months of joining the organization, and after I had attempted without being obsequious (fawning) to develop a professional rapport, I was bluntly cut off (ghosted) from any form of meaningful conversation with Gazlen. However, not before he had requested information/debriefing about technical instruments with which he should have been completely familiar, given his training and senior graduate education! About this time, he began assertive "friendly" advances towards Jillian a support worker, recently divorced, lonely and socially isolated.

Before going on, some background information. Gazlen had been married five times, his current marriage was an "open marriage" by anyone's observations, and Gazlen had already disclosed this fact to a few staff he trusted.

His advances towards the support worker progressed over the course of a year, both people proclaiming it was only a friendship; however, the staff had distinct doubts by that time! So what, you say, office romances are a reality, mind your business! Unfortunately, office politics are office politics, and they can be utterly detrimental to the morale of the organization!.

Case in point, at the Christmas party during his second year, he arrived with his wife of seventeen years, who sat beside him at the banquet table and was by all accounts a lovely person. His "friend" Jillian the support staff female, happened to be sitting across from them. She got up, walked around the table, and asked the man sitting beside Gazlen's wife to "move over please," which he did, allowing Jillian to sit beside Gazlen. This did not bode well as the evening progressed and the drinks flowed. Gazlen's wife became a "third wheel," being eased out of the conversation, which made her look the fool! This scene caused major office gossip during the next few weeks. Gazlen was non-committal and went about his business, but by this time he started demanding a reduced caseload. Actually, this recent change in work-load was requested by his wife in a hand written note to the office manager. The office manager, being a garrulous (talkative) person, asked, "Who wears the pants in the family, Gazlen?" Gazlen's response: "She does!" In point of fact, his now diminutive caseload, approximately two-thirds full-time, affected the profit margin of the clinic and jeopardizing the support staff's annual pay raise.

As time progressed and during Gazlen's last year at the organization, his behavior became more confrontational, imposing his opinion on how the therapist sub-contractors should run their respective business practices within the organization. He approached me twice, challenging the manner in which I ran my operation, implying it was contravening the current and past conventional practice standards of the industry! When I defended myself, Gazlen sloughed it off and left my office, which was more spacious than his; this point I'm sure infuriated him. In time, as you will read, his vindictive behavior escalated towards me. When the owner of the business was told of Gazlen's behavior, he was shocked but did *not* intervene effectively in my opinion. Of note: this gentleman owned the business and his passive behavior towards Gazlen's conduct, gave a "green light" to continue what became grossly inappropriate behavior. It was and is an abrogation of responsibility by an owner *not* to step forward to resolve these situations. Over time, Gazlen's behavior escalated in leaps and bounds! Due, in fact, to no definitive boundaries being drawn by the owner/operator.

Three incidents occurred several months apart, which in my humble opinion would *not* have happened if earlier intervention had been imposed! Gazlen had become increasingly frustrated with the organizational protocol and attempted to impose his will, either through veiled threats beginning with insidious, contemptuous smiles when he passed you, to outright aggressive posturing. For instance, at one point as I walked towards him and then past him at the entrance of the building, he said, "Drive carefully, I wouldn't want you to end up under a truck going home," while smiling that insidious smile and with an aggressive posture (leaning forward encouraging a retaliation)! Later in the year, he, in collusion with his friend, Jillian the support worker, took client files (without permission) from the organization. For what purpose? We didn't find out and I contacted my lawyer about this highly irregular conduct. I was informed that unless this was written as a job duty in his contract, it was breaching professional ethics and could in fact be tantamount to theft of business property. In this regard client files are technically "owned" by the business unless the client has provided written authorization allowing Gazlen's type of transaction to occur. Upon investigation with the administrative director, I was told Gazlen did *not* have anything in writing allowing this to happen. I subsequently wrote a debriefing of the lawyer's response and shared it with the business owner, leaving the matter in his hands. He said he would certainly look into it. The outcome was less than tepid; I was *not* debriefed of the eventual consequences to Gazlen's delinquent behavior, nor was anyone else to my knowledge. Another fumble by the owner, but let me proceed.

There were many more instances such as these but the most outrageous is next. A few weeks before Gazlen gave a brief, barely two-week resignation letter to the owner, the following occurred. Gazlen, while talking on the phone in the middle of the doorway between the subcontractor offices and the front administrative office, was impeding forward progress of anyone wanting to proceed through the doorway. As I tried to walk past him, he blindsided me WITH A BODYCHECK. Outweighed by sixty plus pounds, I was thrown sideways approximately two feet, but maintained balance and kept walking through the doorway, without retaliating in word or action. Why you ask? I knew he was expecting a verbal if not physical retaliation; the second choice could have caused a highly contentious scandal if it got out to the public via gossip, the papers, etetera, especially given our professional standing. I interpreted his behavior as a premeditated attempt to provoke an aggressive retaliation, thus setting me and the business up. In my interpretation, his conduct had malicious intent; maybe he had had a bad day, who knows, but his behavior breached the country's criminal code of conduct, and is considered assault without just cause.

I asked the staff if they saw his bodycheck and no one came forward confirming they witnessed anything. They were only ten feet away. In essence, it would be his word against mine, therefore a legal stand-off; this man was not stupid! Frequently thereafter, I asked the staff if they saw his bodycheck, and no one ever came forward to confirm they'd witnessed anything untoward. Does this guy skate on water or what!?

Lastly, I summarize Gazlen's behavior as such: His persona and general narcissistic conduct employed cruelty and malicious contempt for professionals he assessed as inferior in intellect, training, and/or calculated shrewdness. He "deserted" his position by serving a very short notice and returned to his former job. This he had stated he would never do when he first arrived at our organization two years earlier. To my knowledge, he is still employed at his former job with no plans to retire in the near future.

I invite you to complete the Psychopathy Spectrum Test for Gazlen. When you have completed the test, compare your results with the author's test results at the back of the book under the heading "Author's Test Results – Fifteen Vignettes."

Vignette 10: Mr. Macabeus

In the 1980s, my colleague owned and operated seventeen mental health group homes for adolescents who were "in care" as involuntary admissions due to breaching the child welfare act. By and large, these were very dangerous offenders despite not yet attaining adult status.

Nevertheless, their actions were in many cases so egregious (notably bad) that they required institutionalization and/or a "step down" facility in the community with a high staff complement. My colleague's organization provided a viable option. However, you can imagine the potential problems if one or more of the clients deserted without permission and "acted out" in the community, often at the risk of civilian life or livelihood! A media frenzy would occur, the outcome often at the expense of the organization's well-earned reputation. This outcome happened irregularly, but enough that the staff had to be on guard twenty-four hours per day, both physically and emotionally, which was VERY DRAINING.

Over time, my colleague's high profile group home organization became well known, with a reputation for accepting the "toughest of the tough" juvenile offenders and accepting the risks of treating this clientele in a community setting. Please keep in mind, very few organizations would take on this risky responsibility with such a challenging clientele.

One of the staff members, let's call him Mr. Macabeus, was promoted to the second-in-charge supervisory position. However, as was much later determined, he had manufactured his resumé to state he held an undergraduate degree (he had a high school diploma with mediocre grades) as well as embellishing his past accomplishments in this particular field of mental health social service. Of note: His presenting features were generally outrageous! Forget casual attire, Mr. Macabeus's slovenly appearance was in polite terminology, an outlier to the average person's dress code. In plain English, his appearance did *not* reflect a professional decorum in the least and he often "looked like a slob" as described by his subordinates. In fact, it greatly reduced the credibility of the organization when he presented at conferences or when interacting one on one with colleagues from other agencies. More specifically, scuffed shoes, oversized pants, sport's jackets two sizes too large.

He also had body odour, incredibly decayed teeth, and bad breath. At the age of thirty-five he was not long to live without a major change in quality of life and work life. He often consumed, as observed by his staff, twenty ounces of hard liquor throughout the work day (vodka, to mask any odour) when overly stressed. This caused major problems when support staff phoned him for advice and by the fact that he was required to be on-call duty, twenty-four hours per day!! Looking back Mr. Macabeus must have had an angel on his shoulder!

In his defense, would the average professional want to be employed in this work milieu, with the inherent danger of being harmed by a very dangerous clientele!? Physical intervention was a daily occurrence, which could result in minor to major injury. A learning curve was approximately six months for the uninitiated rookie staff member, many leaving because of their own mental health problems. Why you ask? Ruminating about their safety was a big factor in diminishing their stamina, confidence, and fortitude! Yet, WHY WAS MR. MACABEUS HIRED in the first place, as did many people in the professional community, and later, the family members of the clientele of the organization!

An easy answer would be the incredibly naïve and stupid leadership, but it wasn't that easy. As stated above, this was a very dangerous environment to work in; very few people lasted over four years. The staff were often attacked violently and/or received threats of retaliation by the clientele if their requests were not heeded. This threatening and abusive environment was a draining experience to put it mildly. Yet some staff enjoyed the challenge, and over time the satisfaction of observing positive change in some clients' behavior was enough incentive to stay at the job. But in general, staff turn-over was ongoing, and keeping staff morale required a miracle of regular and intense support, such as cajoling, and providing an expectation of advancement to a different level of the organization's infrastructure, basically away from "front line" work.

This is where Mr. Macabeus's skill set lay! He was street smart, ferociously charming when needed, but also incredibly ruthless in retaliatory behavior if he felt demeaned. When a staff signed the working contract, Mr. Macabeus made it clear that he "owned them." In his words, "In this difficult field many are called yet few are chosen. Are you ready and capable for this adventure?" The young and naïve rookies looked upon his statement as a challenge they could engage in and handle over time (I'm sorry to say a great many didn't make the grade).

In conjunction, his ability to temper the mood of the professional group within the organization was dual purpose. He could "crack the whip" when he felt it was needed, yet be incredibly supportive when he felt it was in the best interest of the organization (and his paycheck). In his mind the staff, was the staff, was the staff. In essence, there would always be infrastructure problems that would affect the morale of the group as a whole, so let's get on with the job at hand and let bygones be bygones! I imagined that in the owner's mind, Mr. Macabeus's innate abilities counteracted the negative aspects of his personality and physical liabilities. A dreadful rationalization, but let's proceed.

Over a period of twelve years—yes, he lasted that long, Mr. Macabeus became a financial business partner with shares in the business and therefore his power expanded to allow him to make decisions, some good, but most very bad! My colleague, the primary owner, frequently turned a blind eye, which unfortunately meant he regularly had to put out political fires that were caused by Mr. Macabeus. Another major problem was the staff selection, an increasing number of large-framed males who used muscle before brains to resolve problems and restore safety within the client population. Yes, you got it right, Mr. Macabeus oversaw all hiring responsibilities as well, which included: hiring, firing, and coordinating the policy procedures of the organization and making sure they were followed (kind of). He was given a lot of power, to put it mildly.

The clientele as stated above, was VERY short-fused, quick to temper, and often retaliated with physical aggression. They could be incredibly vindictive, their "code of the jungle," as stated by one of the staff. Over time, complaints were brought forward by the community, which subsequently reached the media and diminished greatly the reputation of the organization and subsequent referrals by the government agencies and private sector. As a consequence, families were left to deal with a delinquent, often dangerous offender in their household. This demise of the organization's quality control, quality improvement and internal/external customer satisfaction was to rear its ugly head for a number of years during the organization's decline.

During this period, Mr. Macabeus was hospitalized with an enlarged liver, his extramarital affairs resulted in an acrimonious divorce with him losing most, if not all, of his financial investments, including his house. His children deserted him, and the organization's staff, without any form of competent leadership to provide more consistency and follow-up, began to sexually "act out" with the clientele. At one point, after several complaints to the agency's licensing body, there was a very thorough evaluation of the organization in toto, which included the operational infra structure of all seventeen group homes. The owner was told by the ministry, in no uncertain terms, to "shape up or ship out." It was his last warning, as the organization had been under increasing scrutiny during the previous five years. Rival agency complaints about the organization's diminished capabilities added fuel to the fire, further causing its eventual demise.

But I digress, back to Mr. Macabeus. Upon return to work from the hospital, Mr. Macabeus was finally given the "golden handshake" by my colleague, the owner. Unfortunately, my colleague was locked into a long-term contract with Mr. Macabeus due to his financial contributions with two of the group homes, and therefore he remained —albeit at arm's length—in a business relationship with the owner. Mr. Macabeus kept this financial arrangement going for the better part of ten years, supplementing his physical disability pensions and eventual government and work pensions. Unbelievable but true.

Lastly, in the late 2000s, two former group home clients from the early 1980s submitted a joint lawsuit for "gross negligence and unprofessioal conduct" which amounted to several million dollars against the organization, which by this time had been disbanded after the owner's death. Mr. Macabeus was named as a major respondent of this legal action which currently (2024) is still awaiting a judge's decision regarding court action.

I invite you to complete the Psychopathy Spectrum Test for Mr. Macabeus. When you have completed the test, compare your results with the author's test results at the back of the book under the heading "Author's Test Results – Fifteen Vignettes."

Vignette 11: Mr. Bogus Professional

A short one, you need a breather.

One day in the late 1980s, a colleague named Kerry J. told me a stunning yarn which was factually a true story. It had hit the newspapers in the Midwest ten years previously, back in the mid-late 1970s and is still hard to fathom. A foreign individual had successfully competed for a clinical position at a remote rural hospital. In those days, it appeared Human Resources was more lax than current times and did not thoroughly investigate foreign qualifications. The person in question, let's call him Mr. Bogus Professional, had placed on his wall an advanced degree from another country which was written in Latin, as was his license to practice clinical psychology. People simply presumed he was as competent as his curriculum vitae stated, and, oh that fancy diploma must mean he's a qualified person! In defense, this was a small rural city of 25,000 inhabitants whose employment was primarily in the farming industry. It was not a popular location, being situated in a cold, remote area of the country.

Within three months, the "jig was up," as the multidisciplinary team had more than frequently witnessed his blatant, incompetent professional conduct through the one-way mirror and realized they had been conned, duped, manipulated, you name it, "we've been had." The person in question's report writing, if you want to call it that, was storytelling at minimal best. What to do!? Mr. Bogus Professional's licensing body was contacted, a complaint lodged by the administrator of the hospital and director of clinical services, which reflected the severity of the problem! An investigation of sorts was held at which time, due to Mr. Bogus Professional's country of origin being halfway around the world and the urgency of information being sent and period of time for a response being in question, a decision was made to forgo a long and tedious investigation, which most likely violated Mr. Bogus Professional's rights. Whatever, he was terminated "with just cause," provided a six-month severance, escorted off the premises and disallowed from ever practicing in this professional jurisdiction again. It's over you say, the good guys won, this imposter never to be seen again, or so it was thought!? NOT QUITE.

Approximately eighteen months later, Kerry J. said that a colleague of his, who had known Mr. Bogus Professional through collegial connections and the outcome of this clinical disaster, happened to be walking down the corridor of a hospital three hundred miles away. Suddenly, he thought he saw Mr. Bogus Professional walking out of the Human Resources Department!? As the entrance to this particular office was crowded and still thirty yards away, Kerry J.'s colleague couldn't catch up to the man in question, who by this time was almost out of sight. Kerry J.'s colleague arrived at the door, and after waiting in line for a period of time, entered the office and proceeded to fabricate a story about the person in question being an old colleague from many years earlier—but unfortunately, he couldn't remember the man's name.

"The guy with an accent who left in a hurry about thirty minutes ago?" the admin assistant asked.

"Yes, you got it, I forgot his name and want to surprise him; he'll be so happy to see me."

Her response, and brace yourself: "John Davis, his name is John Davis and his office is down the hall and to the right, room 228."

Kerry J.'s colleague literally raced down the hall, and as he approached room 228 he rehearsed what he was going to say in a robust, prosecutorial lawyer voice. He then mustered his resources and knocked on the door! A familiar, foreign, clipped accent responded, "Just a moment," and a second later the door opened, at which time— without going into detail regarding the subsequent discussion Kerry J.'s colleague read a phony "riot act," which described misrepresentation of a professional title, fraud, intention to commit fraud after the fact, etcetera. He subsequently informed this so-called "qualified professional"—or more accurately, bogus professional fraudster—that he was telephoning the Licensing Board and then the police. When he returned, Mr. Bogus Professional, now in a state of shock, confessed that he had legally changed his name to "Westernize" it. This done because of his "inability to successfully compete for interviews and potential gainful employment in this country!"

I BEG YOUR PARDON. He forgot to state the extreme disregard for the clientele he mismanaged who could be potentially traumatized by his malpractice of professional standards!

He did not mention the fact that he had already lost his professional license to practice in this jurisdiction using his "real" name. Talk about denial, rationalization, and minimization. Unbelievable! Bring in the men in blue!

The story hit the newspapers big time. Mind you, no one at that time took the next step to aggressively evaluate the protocol of the Examining Board's assessment of Mr. Bogus Professional's equivalency in professional credentials and capabilities to practice competently! It was many, many years later that a reciprocal agreement, linking geographical regions of the country, was ratified by the various licensing bodies of his profession! How many fraudulent professionals slipped undetected into North America in those days, and how many continue to still practice today AND at the public's risk is anyone's guess.

I invite you to complete the Psychopathy Spectrum Test for Mr. Bogus Professional. When you have completed the test, compare your results with the author's test results at the back of the book under the heading "Author's Test Results – Fifteen Vignettes."

Vignette 12: The Gentleman Hockey Player

During my two-year experience as a Social Assistance caseworker in the late 1970s, I was on duty during lunch hour completing a four-week rotation. One particular day, a gentleman entered the building, approached the intake room where I was stationed, and then waited patiently to be seen for an assessment of fifteen-day emergency Social Assistance.

Two admin assistants appraised the man's appearance and made an unfortunate snap judgment. More specifically, they decided that he was unsavory and was probably out to "bilk the system." Unfortunately, their rude manner and extreme bias made their prejudice obvious to both my client and myself! I took them aside and stated in no uncertain words my disappointment in their professional deportment and to "straighten up their acts" or I'd get the boss involved! Good old-fashioned confrontation sometimes wins the day, and it did that day, or so I thought! The two admin assistants stopped their behavior and walked away in a huff. The gentleman sat there quietly watching, and a very subtle smile crossed his mouth. Later on, he told me he thought I'd said, "Stick out your racks" instead of "Straighten out your acts." I laughed at his misunderstanding but ate my words later on! He was eventually identified as a multiple fraudster in the social assistance network, but on with the story.

The client's turn came shortly thereafter, and one of the admin assistants ushered him into the intake room and chair opposite my desk. As I recall he was wearing an old-fashioned, weather-beaten leather jacket with a hockey insignia. The jacket was so old the leather had cracked and the fading color was not red but ochre. Almost disguising the name sewn below the decal was an emblazoned crest just visible, "MONTREAL CANADIENS." I was mildly curious but held back questions regarding the nature of the jacket until after the application had been completed. I assessed his "financial needs" and found the gentleman eligible to receive fifteen days emergency Social Assistance. This would carry him through to his next government paycheck, no big deal, you say, until I asked him about the jacket and how he acquired it.

The gentleman, by now in his mid-seventies, told me a startling yarn that seemed to be believable—believable can be different than true, I might add. Here he was, sitting directly across from me, talking with little if any hesitation, facial appearance relaxed and at times poised before making an important point; he appeared to be in his realm. The gentleman hockey player said he had played professional hockey for twelve years during the 1920s and '30s, on three different teams. He stated he had been one of the hockey players who carried the great Howie Morenz off the ice (1937) after Morenz was violently checked and sustained a broken leg, from which he never recovered, dying of blood poisoning three weeks later. Of note: Howie Morenz was the Wayne Gretzky of his era.

The older gentleman's stories about professional sports in the 1920s and '30s were from the perspective of an above-average journeyman hockey player. The way he characterized himself were the exact words my sources later on described his skill set and talent on the ice. Whether this was the same individual from that era, or simply a man impersonating this journeyman with the same name and in the same general age bracket, is anyone's guess. Unfortunately, we often interviewed clients with phony identification in the late seventies, computer networking was in its infancy. However, as I think back, his ID indicated he might have been legit, by name and date of birth at least.

Of note: Back in the '70s, each county had its own Social Assistance program, which did not have a sophisticated linkage system with other social support systems. Keep this fact in mind.

Over the course of almost one hour, his candor grew on me and I began to realize he was an enormously gifted raconteur, and I found him simply a "good guy, a straight shooter" as they say! But what had happened over the years? He had the usual stock answers I had heard many, many times from people who were down and out (e.g., bankruptcy, alcoholism, bad divorce). Nevertheless, he had an aura of immense dignity about playing professional hockey back in the day, when there were no multi-million-dollar contracts, and you played simply for the love of the game. I asked him where he was living, and he said in a northern city most of the time, but during the summer months would return to this area to pick fruit, catch up with his friends, and make, in his words, "a pot full of dough," which was in those days approximately fifty to seventy dollars per day. He also stated his philosophy of life: "Yeah, I've had my ups and downs, but compared to other guys I've had it pretty good, no complaints, a loving wife who recently passed away, two children and three grandchildren."

He went on to discuss two friends who were veterans of WW2 and roomed down the hall from him in the "seedy" center town hotel where he lived during the "picking season." His friends were veterans of the WW2 Battle of Dieppe, a precursor to D-Day. Both had been teenagers lying about their age when they signed up, wanting to see some "action" as recently trained American Rangers (commandos). One of the friends had been in the second wave of landing crafts, loaded with troops heading towards the beach, and unfortunately witnessed the carnage. When the landing craft's ramp was dropped, he was immediately hit with machine gun fire and fell into the water. One of his buddies, a troopmate—apparently one of his dearest friends, both in boot camp and later on living in barracks—dragged him onto the beach. At this point the friend was killed. After lying in the sand feigning death, the Gentleman hockey player's friend was quickly captured by the Germans, sent to a hospital to convalesce, and then placed in a prisoner of war camp until 1945. Three long years waiting for war to end.

The second veteran friend had been on a landing craft in the third wave, which got to within one thousand yards of the beach, saw first-hand the carnage and that the battle was irretrievable, and was forever thankful the landing craft was ordered back to the ship! This veteran, although not wounded physically, was mentally scarred after witnessing the slaughter on the beach. The trauma of that day, witnessing the slaughter on the beach for less than an hour until the landing craft was ordered back to the ship, had indeed changed his life! At the time of this story, in the late 1970s the friends were not yet sixty years of age. Both men met in a convalescent hospital in a large city after the war, both men became hopeless alcoholics, both men lived off Social Assistance and Federal Government Veterans Allowance, and both men currently survived day-to-day eating dog food in this "seedy" downtown hotel.

So, when the gentleman hockey player finished his story, he noticed my eyes had become moist, requiring me to blink rapidly to stem any tears. He then said, and I remember this distinctly, "I see you haven't lived much of this life, bud. It only gets better, don't think about the past, think about the future and do your best." ("Doing *what?*" was my rhetorical question.)

To be fair to the reader, I may bias your assessment with my final observations; interpret them as you wish. After talking with me, the gentleman hockey player engaged in a discussion with one of my older colleagues about the nature of emergency funds being provided. At the time, my colleague was looking down reviewing the application. Simultaneously, I noticed the gentleman hockey player's facial features become rigid with a cold, disconcerting, directed gaze. As my colleague appeared to be finishing his review of the document, the gentleman hockey player's facial features changed markedly to a relaxed, charming "everyone's buddy" expression, a 180-degree reversal of behavior! Later, as he walked out of the building, he waved, while putting the check into his pocket before turning the corner a few yards from our door.

The two support workers approached me and laughed, saying in hushed tones, "Why did you shut us up, Jake?" and walked away, never to let me forget my naiveté.

Days later, we were contacted by another Social Assistance Center after they noticed my business card had fallen from Mr. Gentleman Hockey Player's Montreal Canadiens jacket. It's all in a day's work!

I invite you to complete the Psychopathy Spectrum Test for The Gentleman Hockey Player. When you have completed the test, compare your results with the author's test results at the back of the book under the heading "Author's Test Results – Fifteen Vignettes."

Vignette 13: Fred

During the early-mid 1970s, I met Fred, a senior graduate student at the local university, which I had attended as an undergraduate a few years earlier. He had been married for several years, and as I got to know him, I noticed he was a very heavy drinker. The Dr. Jekyll/ Mr.Hyde personality fit his behavior to a T when he was under the influence. Contributing to his need to self-medicate was the intensity and duration of his graduate studies, which placed him under enormous pressure during the three years I knew him and his wife Jill.

As I recollect, Fred and Jill had met while both worked at a correction institute in another country. They had a relatively short courtship before marriage, and to my knowledge, Jill was unaware of Fred's drinking problem throughout their courtship. I observed Fred's behavior when he was drunk; he'd often become quite menacing. His uncle had taught him the rudiments of boxing, and he demonstrated his ability on the heavy bag a few times, enough to let me know his potential to settle matters quickly and ruthlessly. As stated, he had a "flip side" to his personality, especially when placed under pressure, which caused him to drink heavily. This usually occurred on weekends, however, alcohol was always at "arm's length" throughout the week. "To relax my nerves," he said on many occasions.

Over time, I tended to rationalize Fred's drinking problem as a result of being constantly stressed by the pressures of graduate school. However, I soon realized I was sorely mistaken, and by this time a friendship had developed with this couple and I was invited to visit their hometown, which consisted of several million citizens with the usual array of denizens (inhabitants) of a city of that size. Basically, you grew up tough if you wanted to survive.

At one point, I met Fred's father, now living in the family's winterized cottage in a rural area, with his second wife, who was his former administration assistant. This gentleman at first glance, looked ten years older than his stated age and had a tendency to exaggerate his success in business. He was disheveled and dropped the "F bomb" consistently. I later found out his business acumen in his chosen field had been a dismal failure bordering on financial disaster. I'm guessing alcohol was a major contributor to his downfall, but then what did I know.

During the two-hour interaction with his son, Fred, there was a role reversal of father-son behavior. Fred easily antagonized his father with a frivolous sense of humor, poking fun with innuendos about his father's many failures including: business decisions gone bad; divorcing his wife and leaving the family to fend for itself; Fred's father forced to move to the "wasteland" where he currently resided, and many other examples I fail to remember. During these interactions Fred enjoyed overwhelming his father during his attempts at retaliation. That led to further abuse of his father's manhood, at which time the gentleman began to drink more heavily to cushion the barrage of insults. I was worried it would continue to escalate, until his father's wife put a stop to it: "Gentleman, shut the f . . . up, it's time for supper."

Everyone gathered around the dinner table, and that was that. Nice introduction to Fred's family life!? Jill where were you during your courtship with this man called Fred!?

Upon returning to this country, I learned that Fred's scholastic colleague had failed to have his thesis accepted by his supervisor, which was a requirement before it was sent to his defense committee. This setback caused everyone concern—except Fred, his so-called friend! Fred shrugged his shoulders and sighed, "Many are called, few are chosen, Jake," and finished the night drinking to his friend's academic demise.

By this time, and after the "vacation" with Fred and his wife, I became more fearful of the inner workings of this man. I lived the next floor up and was in daily contact, by the fact of walking by their apartment to get to my place and being invited in for a drink with Fred, all the while thinking, *When will it be my turn at the guillotine!?*

To digress, at no time during the three-year relationship did I confront this man's ignorant behavior, knowing his retaliation would be five- and even ten-fold in magnitude. In Fred's mind, the demeaning behavior was warranted by the fact that YOU HAD THE AUDICITY to confront his oversized ego!! You weren't just punished verbally, you were humiliated, taunted with veiled threats, and left to pick up the pieces.

Later on, when I moved to a nearby city to complete further scholastic studies, I invited Fred and Jill to see the house my roommate and I had rented. We had flipped a coin to see who would take over the "study room"; the loser would have to study in the kitchen or his bedroom. I won the toss. When Fred saw the study room which was now my domain, he instantly started verbal darts that led to outright insults of my integrity while living upstairs for three years as a former neighbor. Nice guy, huh.

Moving on, Fred knew which side his bread was buttered on in his academic program, inviting the department head for dinner and wine many times, and achieving what appeared to be a very favorable relationship. What's wrong with that, you say. Once again, when the professor left these evening arrangements, Fred's malicious tendency to victimize people who were either weak, not present, or threatening, became an onslaught of caustic innuendos, and if you attempted to quell his aggression, it was turned on you once again, five- to ten-fold in magnitude! Never, ever was an apology provided, and many times he would remind you of his inordinately high I.Q. and ability to "crush you like an ant."

I'm sure you're asking, "Why did his wife Jill stay in this relationship!?" Fred's behavior did not exhaust Jill until much later in the marriage. More specifically: after Fred *failed* at his studies due to laziness—and I'm sure over-drinking didn't help. Fred was then required to look for a regular job to make a living, as Jill had supported him for five plus years while he attended graduate school. He failed to reduce his alcohol consumption, which I'm told was way out of control. That's when he allegedly became more physically violent, and threats of instant reprisal would occur if Jill retaliated. She stayed, and stayed, AND STAYED in this domestic fiasco for a further two years. A brilliant example of the battered woman syndrome. I personally witnessed the tricyclic, three-stage behavior in this co-dependent relationship, that is: tension building, acute acting out, and loving-contrite stages, and these rotated throughout the three years I was their "friend."

I did not hear about Fred and Jill for a further two years, until I bumped into a mutual friend in a bar, who happened to work in the same city as me. She said Jill had helped Fred to get a teaching job at a community college, at which time he began an affair with a student ten years his junior. When he was caught and faced losing 50 percent of his possessions through divorce settlement, he pleaded stress problems and vowed he would leave his paramour (mistress). This didn't happen, I bet you're not surprised. Finally, Jill dumped Fred once and for all after he not-so-secretly returned to his paramour to continue the affair.

That was the last I heard of the couple for approximately five years. Once again, I bumped into the mutual friend at the same bar, and she provided an update on the Fred and Jill saga. Jill had remarried several years after divorcing Fred, this time to a successful lawyer, and they had a daughter. The lawyer had met Fred once, and asked our mutual friend, "What did you think of Fred when you knew him?"

"I thought he was a f . . . a . . . !" she replied.

The story doesn't end, Fred apparently joined a major pharmaceutical company, and over the years rose in the ranks and made a killing financially!

I invite you to complete the Psychopathy Spectrum Test for Fred. When you have completed the test, compare your results with the author's test results at the back of the book under the heading "Author's Test Results – Fifteen Vignettes."

Vignette 14: Dybuk

I have provided a preamble to Vignette 14, the next and second-last vignette. The rationale for this is that I'd like to set the proverbial stage. Then . . . hang on to your hats while you listen to the tale of this individual's conduct!

Preamble

Strategic planning is a set of activities meant to help an organization change to meet some designated outcome or goal. The achievement of the goal cannot be realized without some mid-course corrections. Strategic plans are visions of where an organization wants to go, and some changes may be made in order for the objectives to be achieved. Specifically, an organization may be forced to reduce/remove some of the old processes in order to increase efficiency/effectiveness. To accomplish these new objectives, short-term goals are set as "markers" to guide the proper movement/behavior toward a longer-term goal. In conjunction, as Burnham (1995) states, strategic plans are visions of the future of the organization's plan of action, and are commonly shared among the members of the organization.

Keep this preamble in mind as you read the following description of a senior mid manager's conduct working within the bureaucracy of a respected organization.

My introduction to the next individual was in the early 2000s, and it was eventful to say the least! There I was, standing amongst a group of colleagues when a short, intense man approximately ten years older than us proceeded to bully his way through the group to discuss an issue with one of my colleagues. No introductions were made, but as they say, a picture is worth a thousand words. The interloper (intruder) was a senior mid manager in the organization, trained at one of the top five institutions in the country, and he let everyone know this fact.

The four characteristics of the Dark Tetrad entered my mind, and for an instant I experienced déjà vu from previous trauma. *Oh no*, I thought, *I hope I don't cross this guy's path in the future!*

At that time, the recipient of the intruder's attention had just completed an advanced degree and was leaving the organization for another job, a promotion, actually, and as it turned out, I was his replacement. At the end of his discussion with the interloper, my colleague turned to me and introduced this individual who we can call Dybuk. A silly nickname, but one that described this man's behavior to a T (there's that expression again)! Over the next few years, I was unfortunate enough to witness outlandish behavior that should have caused senior management significant loss of sleep, heart palpitations, advanced aging, strategic changes in policy and procedure. Nope, Dybuk lasted until HE decided to leave and took another job across town. Some background information follows.

Group meetings, which included ten different professions, were his forté, and he used every trick in the book to boost his egotistical, self-indulgent behavior and alpha male presence. It became so bad that at one point the staff had pre-arranged to leave en masse if Dybuk crossed the line of unprofessional conduct one more time. He did just that, and staff retaliated, walking out during a heated debate. Later on, they suffered for this act of retaliation. He did *not* suffer fools gladly and surmised quickly who the ringleaders of this "plot" were and complained vociferously to senior management. Within six months they were transferred, or in some cases fired, under what many felt were trumped-up allegations. Quite frankly, from my perspective, THEY WERE trumped up allegations. Remember, Dybuk was a powerful man, highly regarded by his professional peers and very competent at his job, according to his rating by senior management. This contradicted the general consensus by staff who were wondering how long this absurdity would last, but in senior management's minds they were lucky to have Dybuk. Or so they thought! One last significant issue to include: this was NOT a union shop.

Dybuk was a lady's man, and with his salary, debonaire manner, and good looks, he quickly seduced willing participants in his amorous game of seek and conquer. Unfortunately, his bachelor lifestyle became somewhat hampered—he was married, with a four-year-old boy, and was caught red-handed by his wife after one of his flings. Believe it or not, his wife had passed him on the highway while he was out driving his outrageously expensive convertible sports car, with his newly conquered fling rustling his hair. This occurred while returning from one of his rendezvous locations, after telling his wife an emergency had arisen out of town, and he would return after the weekend.

This scandal was the last straw, causing divorce proceedings. Shortly thereafter, Dybuk had one of his flings from a conference in another country take him up on contacting him, "if ever in town," and it happened! Six months after meeting this individual, a knock came to the conference room door, at which time he was involved in a very serious budget matter with senior management. He answered the door and was met with a surprise. "Hi, Dybuk, I took you up on your invitation, let's go out later on." I'm sure he was trying to remember who this person was!?.

Later on, his propensity to seduce younger, and I mean much younger, women occurred closer to his job at the organization. He was on twenty-four-hour call as a senior advisor during forest fire season, and one of his jealous lovers informed on him. Simply put, she disclosed he had devised a rotation schedule for late night "meetings" with his girlfriends at two-hour intervals, in the lounge room at the rear of the building. This information eventually got around the various departments of the organization. An inquiry occurred and determined that over several years he had "trained" fifty-seven participants to engage in this late evening schedule of "meetings," without management being the wiser. How did this go unnoticed, you ask? Unfortunately, once again, senior management had "deaf ears." This man was Svengali with a highly developed libido. Please read on!

As it happened, Dybuk had one subordinate staff member who was a "friend," believe it or not. Unfortunately, the friend found himself involved in a boxing match with this miscreant. Dybuk, it appeared, was a very adept fist fighter, having been raised in Ireland. This WAS NOT a sparring session after an evening of drinking and carousing downtown. His friend became a human punching bag and showed up at our weekly meeting with dark sunglasses camouflaging a black eye and swollen cheekbones; it was not pretty. A few months later, Dybuk's name was quoted in a newspaper article alleging defrauding Federal income tax of 1.5 million dollars, which he challenged and won a significant reduction in taxes owed. Yet throughout all the hoopla, he kept his job within the organization and was not alarmed in the least of his notoriety. It reinforced his gigantic ego that he could do no wrong and get away with anything, or so it seemed case after case. Senior management did nothing to challenge this egregious behavior to our knowledge, certainly during my employment, anyway! The amazed staff ascertained the board's rationale for their passive approach and consistent lack of intervention was "it's his personal business and none of our concern." This caused frivolous and caustic statements by the staff to buttress their rising disdain.

"By the way, he is very competent at his job isn't he."

"Is there a bus nearby, let's take it for a joy ride when Dybuk is out jogging."

Quite frankly, who knows what the board's rationale was for keeping him employed over the years.

Lastly, he finally got tired of his current job and successfully competed for a significant increase in salary and job promotion at another organization across town. A few months later, during a conference I was attending sponsored by his new organization, I literally bumped into him as I left the dining area. He threw his arms around me and said, "Hey, we've got to get together sometime! Anytime you need a reference, I'm in the book!"

I invite you to complete the Psychopathy Spectrum Test for Dybuk. When you have completed the test, compare your results with the author's test results at the back of the book under the heading "Author's Test Results – Fifteen Vignettes."

Vignette 15: The Interrogator

Towards the end of my career, I bumped into a former colleague, and after a few drinks he entertained me with his experiences at his former job, which he had recently quit. How could I tell him that I'd experienced far greater catastrophes many, many times in my long career? His problems had begun almost as soon as he arrived at the new job, located in a geographical area far from his previous home. Hence, new customs and different mannerisms with which to become familiar. He had previously lived in a metropolitan, sophisticated city of more than six million and transferred two thousand miles to a Midwestern city of less than 400,000.

His first staff meeting was a series of questions about his background, allowing his colleagues to get an idea of his experience and general competence. It also appeared that his predecessor had left under mysterious circumstances. In conjunction, it seemed one particular team member took an immediate dislike to this recently arrived "newbie," due to the nature of the questions asked by he and the team members. Subsequently, it became obvious, after more than a dozen questions from this team member that the motive was to find areas of weakness, or at least discomfort and then focus a barrage of questions to "test" the newbie's mettle. As my former colleague told me: "I felt like I was being interrogated, rather than interviewed, which put me on the defensive right away." It should be stated that my colleague was competent, had over thirty years of experience, and more than enough knowledge to reduce a staff member's need to demonstrate the confrontational behavior described.

Six months passed, and the interrogator, as we'll call him, had not let up, nor was he eager to develop a cordial professional alliance, even at the most superficial level. My former colleague observed that the interrogator was given a "free hand" by the director of the program (who was soon to retire) to complete his duties mentoring students and junior staff members. In conjunction, he and his cadre of supporter peers, approximately six staff, virtually ran the unit.

My former colleague realized very early on that he and another colleague, also relatively new, were left out of action-planning unit objectives and future optics. Unfortunately, the interrogator's entitled role over the years had *not* been challenged by his peers, who were made to "pick up the slack," carrying the burden of extra job duties and subsequent work load.

According to my former colleague, nothing had been done to correct this biased division of duties during the past ten years or more. The organization politics, being what they were, allowed this discrepancy to continue over time, causing a mild to moderate friction to interfere with working conditions. It was quite evident that the nature of the interrogator's duties WERE HIS DOMAIN, and that was that! His peers had allowed this irresponsible situation to be maintained, and I must state one last time that this was *not* a union shop.

Several issues arose during the following year. The interrogator was observed spending extra time and effort improving the skill sets of the younger female staff members he was mentoring. The other students and junior staff members were wary of challenging this behavior for fear of being poorly evaluated. The interrogator was frequently late for work, arriving at 11 a.m. when his work day started at 8:30 a.m. He completed his duties moderately well when provided encouragement, but his efficiency was taken to task frequently, causing a passive aggressive behavior to surface—as described by my colleague. The interrogator, to be frank, had little to no understanding of the undertakings of his role AS IT SHOULD BE DONE. His tardiness in submitting reports, giving appropriate feedback to correct errors, and currying favor of the young, pretty female subordinates he was supervising, was unprofessional and totally irresponsible according to my former colleague!!

Continuing with this story, my colleague observed that the interrogator's cadre of peers, who'd worked with him for upwards of twenty years, allowed an enmeshed (personal boundaries are unclear) working relationship to occur, which became habituated over time. This greatly impeded the effectiveness of external critical feedback attempting to correct the status quo. In other words, the fox had been in the chicken coop too long!

An example was provided by my former colleague of how this problem was intensified. After the director of the program retired, his position was given on a trial basis to the interrogator. Over a period of several months, he proved to be a catastrophic choice due to his general tardiness in completing paper work and administrative duties required for such an essential position. Unfortunately, his colleagues had to jump in to avoid the ship sinking, which was identified as complicity in reinforcing the problem at hand, more specifically, the interrogator's general incompetence in this role.

In conjunction, the pressure of the job precipitated the interrogator's short fuse, aggressive tone, and surly, condescending behavior; in basic language, he pissed people off! His immaturity manifested in a complete change of wardrobe and hairstyle, which raised significant eyebrows, and reflected a regression in lifestyle. He also frequently rotated a string of girlfriends young enough to be his granddaughters (he was born in 1950), whom he paraded unabashedly to professional forums and national conventions and loved the attention it provided. Needless to say, this Errol Flynn (1940s sex symbol) bohemian behavior did not bode well with senior management! That is, as easygoing as they seemed to be in the past, they were suddenly "switched on," and finally intervened appropriately! The buck stopped at this recent behavior due to "problems" with financial support from the funding organization(s), and according to the gossip mill, senior management receiving phone call complaints regarding his behavior, wardrobe, and general lack of protocol considering his position of authority. Needless to say, Mr. Intrrerrogator was "pressured" out of the organization.

At one point, years later, he and I competed for a position of similar job duties and responsibilities AND HE GOT THE JOB!? I was infuriated, but then Mr. Interrogator had beaten the odds for most of his adult life, hadn't he.

I invite you to complete the Psychopathy Spectrum Test for Mr. Interrogator. When you have completed the test, compare your results with the author's test results at the back of the book under the heading "Author's Test Results – Fifteen Vignettes."

CHAPTER FOUR:

Profiling the Organization Miscreant Within a Unionized Work Environment

The organization, if unionized, can become an easy work environment wherein the organization miscreant can perform misdeeds. In my opinion, it is often difficult to challenge this individual *effectively,* and usually takes a long time to *accurately* identify, categorize, and then document their dysfunctional behavior. Following the documentation, having it processed, debated, and resolved without a lot of "political bloodshed" is difficult! Why, you ask? Because there are so many union rules that can be manipulated to the miscreant's advantage.

If the organization miscreant is *not* management, termination of a *union* employee must be a result of "just cause." This is *not* an easy process in most cases and not infrequently a "cake walk" defense for the organization miscreant—they are that cunning! Especially if any discrepancies have been found in the indictment.

I have witnessed this type of political fiasco frequently, especially during the 1980s and '90s prior to more recent media attention, identifying corporate/organization misdeeds (e.g., Bernie Madoff scandal). The behavior of the organization miscreant in today's work-a-day world is still very difficult to contain. This is certainly the case if allowed to continue their behavior over an extended period of time! The longer they inhabit the work environment, the more skilled they become at using manipulation and guile to achieve their ruthless ends! Keep this in mind as you read on.

Management in these circumstances must *prove* the extremity of the alleged misdeeds. How so you ask? This type of decision-making must go through arbitration or a grievance procedure! Generally speaking, the organization miscreant's predisposition for highly manipulative, cold-blooded behavior, habituated in many cases since early teens, makes them formidable opponents. In basic language they are slick! They frequently exploit existing conflicts between members of their team to mask their own devious intentions. They will often resort to using a token defense such as, "I had to defend myself, I didn't cause this conflict but walked into a cutthroat situation."

This "don't blame me" attitude and subsequent pronouncements to superiors, especially senior administration who request a debriefing, are used frequently to deflect blame against the organization miscreant's reputation as a "true blue" union member (in this wonderful arena to exploit). Some examples include:

"How could you blame me for anything, I'm a hard worker let me provide examples!"

"It's become readily apparent that people are jealous of my abilities, I have to continually watch my back to defend myself."

"Are you KIDDING ME, where did you get that (complaint) from, THEY are the problem not me."

Prior to this sham defense, the organization miscreant has reviewed, digested, and rehearsed any identified loopholes in the organization's operational protocol. From there they've crafted devious plans against staff, management, union representatives—whomever they feel will help them accomplish their twisted agenda, more specifically creating new conflicts! This is done in an effort to develop (in their mind) a safer, more powerful position of authority and control within and external to the organization. Their basic mantra is "upward mobility, upward mobility, upward mobility" (at all costs)! As stated by Clarke (2005), "Their life and work is about self-gratification, they have no reason to change their behavior because people are not happy with the way they are acting" (p. 254).

To emphasize this point, in many organizations the respective employees often work independently and have political agendas that are observed over time by the organization miscreant. As a ploy, the organization miscreant (especially in a management position) will subtly side with *both* conflicting parties having ongoing unresolved issues. In these situations, communication is often masked and indirect, thereby making resolution of the issue(s) more complex to resolve. This discrepancy increases the potential for conflict and subsequent peer pressure to conform with the group majority, who have become burdened by the "trench fighting."

This conflict behavior falls into the political agenda of the organization miscreant! The dynamics of the agenda has been cultivated over time with repeated practice in many varied work situations, using devious ploys to gain control, ploys that have been refined since early adolescence in many cases. The organization miscreant is that cunning, don't be fooled by their claims of union pedigree—morality and ethics are *not* in their game plan! Alternately, if they have reached a management position, depending on their rank (i.e.,mid or senior management) their political "lethality" can increase exponentially.

Of note: It is my understanding, that there has *not* been a research study from reputable sources indicating that true psychopathy, which includes organization miscreants, can be effectively treated with talk therapy. These individuals—to a lesser clinical intensity including sociopaths and subclinical psychopaths—have developed a marked personality disorder, beginning with oppositional defiance in early-mid adolescence, to conduct disorder in later adolescence, which includes callous unemotional (CU) traits and finally, by age eighteen the delinquency of their behavior can be diagnosed as psychopathy. Remember their clinical profile, the Dark Tetrad, which is comprised of:

- Lack of empathy
- Malignant narcissism
- Machiavellian behavior (i.e., back-stabbing)
- Emotional and/or physical sadism

Be wary when observing this behavior syndrome, as it characterizes a group of symptoms that, when occurring together, reflects a particular antisocial abnormality.

In this regard, the organization miscreant's presenting behavior includes the following behavioral repertoire (Clarke 2005, pp.101-111):

- Unethical behavior
- Intolerance/easily bored
- Unpredictable behavior/shallow emotions
- Parasitic behavior
- Undependable and failure to take responsibility for behavior
- Workplace bullying*
- Seeks increased power and control within the company*
- Creates conflict between organization members*
- Interpersonal behavior – deceitfulness/devious/frequent lying; intimidating behavior; charming/superficial manner*

*The highlighted symptoms frequently *increase* over time, often leading to staff exodus from the organization.

I remember a time, while working as a consultant, when twenty-three staff members quit or were fired over a three-year period; the total employment of the organization was less than forty staff. When questioned about the "fallout" by so many employees, the answer revolved around two senior management working in partnership to maintain the status quo they had developed. Any hint of "change" in work protocol meant the "chopping block," and so it happened, over time people got tired and quit, or were pushed out. Both individuals in senior management were in competition to see who was "more powerful in mind and deed," as described by one of the staff members, which reflects what is termed "narcissistic twinning"— competitive behavior between two very cruel individuals, enamoured by the other person's apparent equivalency in ruthless, formidable behavior. As stated, conventional talk therapy simply does *not* work. However, a more *behavioral approach* discussed later in the chapter can impact the organization miscreant's career and pocket book. Using this type of intervention strategy can potentially curb inappropriate conduct, and occasionally influences change (reduction of predatory behavior). Nonetheless, in the writer's experience, these behaviors are deep rooted, and modification—*not* elimination—is rarely achieved in the short run. The nature of change in these cases usually follows a two steps forward, one step back variance over a protracted period of time, if there is any change at all!

Contributing to this problem is a profound need to fulfill their needs regardless of ethics and morality, which is reflected by enormous narcissistic, self-gratifying behavior. Unfortunately, in many cases, the union provides numerous opportunities for this individual to manipulate the environment through a variety of ingenious methods discussed in Chapter 5.

Action Plan by Administration – Identifying Ploys Used Prior to Executive Employment

Continually, throughout the book, I have identified the organization miscreant's pathological need for power and control. Many will attempt to achieve this through administrative senior management positions. As noted, they aggressively achieve these positions through guile, manipulation, and cunning ("street smart" intelligence). In many instances they are able to dupe the executive board with their verbal fluency, although their *depth* of knowledge is often identified as being limited if challenged. Nevertheless, they have refined the "interview game," especially in rural communities or smaller cities where their presentation skills "win the day." More specifically, they use finesse and seductive charm that beguiles the board, which is unfamiliar with such behavior, and generally the board is eager to hire such an "accomplished professional." In the past, early in my career, I was "seduced" several times by this behavior throughout the executive search interview process, as a board member and a consultant in a few situations, enamoured by the miscreant's use of wit, charm, and obvious savvy of interview dynamics. These were potential executive recruits, who were eventually identified as organization miscreants! I must confess their cunning and ruthless manipulation still haunts me today. More specifically, when eventually hired, the charm factor beguiling the staff (in the beginning) and subsequent comfort in using increasingly aggressive ploys over time, to gain greater power as the true nature of their personality was expressed.

Action Plan by Senior Management and Board Executive Versus Ploys of An Organization Miscreant (During Employment)

The organization miscreant has to be *controlled and eventually terminated* once the nature of their pathological behavior is identified!! I hope you identify this as a major priority as overseers at your place of business. More specifically, accomplish a *boundary-specific* threshold of resistance (to be discussed below). This should be done before this conniving individual causes extensive damage to the office personnel and future opportunities for the development of the organization financially.

As stated earlier, *balancing the rights* of the organization miscreant as an employee, and their colleagues' rights within the political infrastructure of the organization is no easy feat. To further highlight this dilemma, Clarke (2005) identifies the issue at hand with the following statement: "Three of the four sub-types of workplace psychopaths exploit or harm their victims in criminal or under-handed ways that *cannot* be managed by the organization on a day-to-day basis. In reality, only the organization psychopath can be managed (day-to-day)"(p.253). Clarke's rationale states: the corporate criminal psychopath, violent criminal psychopath, and the occupational psychopath, are for the most part disciplined by management implementing strategies, *after the fact* (pp.253-54).

In Clarke's book, he documents the following organization policy which is more amenable to controlling *current* inappropriate conduct within the organization. This is implemented by using general management principles under the heading "How to manage the organizational workplace psychopath." His broad-based strategies are as follows (pp. 255-56):

1. Ensure all employees have a safe working environment, free from threat of physical and/or psychological harm;
2. Reduce staff resignation rates by eliminating "antisocial" behavior within the organization;
3. Promote an organizational reputation as a favored employer, encouraging promising and skilled employees to work in the organization, thereby increasing profitability;
4. To increase productivity by reducing or eliminating the negative effects of the organizational psychopath on other employees' work output;
5. To *minimize or eliminate damage* caused to the organization's reputation as a result of unethical, manipulative, or deceptive organizational psychopath work practices.

Management Protection Scheme Versus the Organization Miscreant

The following protocol is an option utilizing *behavioral intervention methods* to "dragnet" a protection protocol throughout the organization. This format is introduced to *reduce* the organization miscreant's efforts at exploitation. As stated many times, this is a very clever and cunning person who quickly identifies incursions by management, which threaten to reduce the miscreant's power brokering efforts, which over time corrupt the organization's operational safety.

More specifically, *a formal protection scheme* (action plan) provides an attempt by management to reduce this person's delinquency within the organization, while at the same time collecting data to defeat the organization miscreant. The success rate is measured by its ability to: a) reduce this individual's need for causing harm, if possible and b) provide a testament of good will by management towards its staff coalition to protect them from harm (if taken to court). Lastly, this intervention process is used to thwart the miscreant's ruthless efforts to gain power and control, and may be enough to cause their exit from the organization. But don't count on it.

Introducing The Action Plan (overview)

Preamble

Develop a co-ordinated plan of action between the membership of the organization and an expert consultant(s) (i.e., forensic psychologist, forensic psychiatrist). The expert(s) should have the composite skills, training, and experience to provide a thorough knowledge base to *decrease* potential errors made by a planning committee.

To reiterate: Hiring the appropriate expert requires a candidate with a requisite level of forensic expertise and experience dealing with psychopathology and organization delinquency. This is sacrosanct (an absolute necessity) in conjunction with the development of a *team approach* to defeat the organization miscreant over time.

As discussed, **the organization miscreant is VERY clever at finding ways and means to infiltrate and subsequently corrupt organization dynamics.** *Counteracting this behavior* is the expert's knowledge, training experience, strength of character in one-to-one confrontations, and ability to develop a powerful team! This hopefully provides a good leverage point which over time lays siege to the organization miscreant's deviant behavior!

Behavior Intervention Strategies

A reinforcement contingency program as described below is often the last resort to attempt to influence change. This may be accomplished through a reward system that makes sense to this individual's narcissistic personality. As previously stated, expert opinion views talk therapy as ineffective due to the miscreant's defense mechanism (e.g., denial, rationalization, projection) being conditioned to meet their narcissistic needs! Conversely, the expert may begin the intervention process by examining a *contingency reward system* to interfere with the past reinforcement strategies used by the miscreant to reinforce their ruthless conduct. There are two types of negative reinforcement (behavior is followed by terminating an unpleasant event) that can be identified in this case: Avoidance Learning and Escape Learning.

Avoidance learning requires the organization miscreant to prevent a negative event from occurring. In this situation, telling the truth negates loss of pay or a potential verbal/written warning placed on their file. The staff will be debriefed by the expert(s) to provide supporting documentation indicating the individual's honesty quotient in these situations. This usually begins on a daily basis and becomes less required as the organization miscreant's deviant behavior is reduced (e.g., less lying over time). Definitions of "honest behavior" and a range of conduct admissible to be counted as "honest" are to be tabulated by the staff over time. A reward system is developed that is documented for *frequency* and *duration*. Yes, it's a lot of work to devise this reinforcement program, but it will hopefully cause a reduction of inappropriate conduct over time. It also provides a solid defense for management's introduction of this protocol, if challenged in court.

Escape learning describes how the organization miscreant learns to escape a situation in order to avoid a negative experience. For instance, being constantly observed and placed on probation for bullying is stopped when the organization miscreant *decreases and eventually eliminates the abusive behavior,* which, by the way, is a long shot from what I've seen in my experience.

A third option (token economy) is often thought of in regard to changing children's behavior. This factor, if actively engaged with the organization miscreant, may be enough to provoke their resignation ("I won't tolerate being treated like a kid!").

The following is an overview of the token economy program:

The organization miscreant is *oriented* regarding the "performance management protocol." Basically, it will allow the individual to achieve goals when they receive a certain number of reward points. *There is no discussion or arbitration about involvement in this intervention process.* Batten down the hatches, folks, for this directive (by administration/expert) reduces any power of influence by the organization miscreant and they will resist this directive with gusto![5]

The method of reinforcement is described below:

Token Economy reinforces appropriate behavior while at the same time punishing undesirable behavior. In this situation the organization miscreant *earns rewards* (e.g., tokens) towards certain things they find desirable to work toward. The token reward process can be effective within the organization milieu when involving such *positive feedback* as optimistic evaluations from staff members and customers/clientele which potentially earn choices which could include: a reduced work schedule, tickets to a sport's game, an extended weekend, or vacation period.

Conversely, reward points are *reduced for inappropriate behaviors* such as: staff complaints, bullying co-workers, tardiness in attendance at meetings, etcetera. All of which have been categorized and collated with the point system and provided to the organizational miscreant at the commencement of the program.

The criteria for token rewards and reductions are determined by the expert and the administration and professional cadre of chosen workers within the organization.

You're probably saying by this time, "Why do we allow this person ANY concessions to learn positive behavior, which should be already established at this stage in their career!?" This particular reinforcement strategy is one example of an attempt by management to reduce the miscreant's inappropriate professional conduct. In future, it can be used as a defense if challenged in court. Remember, these scheming individuals will be ruthless to defend their actions as a rational response to organization malfeasance using such statements as "Due to the dysfunction I encountered at XYZ organization, I had to respond

---

5   Other staff may be placed under the token reward system to reduce suspicions which arise if the organization miscreant is "singled out". Being the only candidate could potentially be used as ammunition in a future harassment lawsuit, initiated by this cunning individual.

aggressively to defend myself" or "Why am I being harassed by the organization when I'm trying to improve staff relations by getting rid of the dead wood" or "TELL ME, when in the past was an employee treated in such a demeaning manner!" These defense mechanisms have been used many times (denial, rationalization, minimization, projection) to maintain their sense of identity and reflecting the narcissistic overlay of their personality.

The token economy reinforcement technique, as stated, is *not* foolproof and has its limitations, primarily the strength of the individual staff members to follow through "to the letter" the appropriate interpretation of what behavior determines which point(s) selection. However, it is worth a try as long as it produces change to more positive behavior by the organization miscreant, thereby reducing staff distress and decreasing the staff's frustration by finally working towards an improved quality of life in the work environment. All of which hopefully reduces staff turnover rates, but again, don't hold your breath!

If the intervention is challenged in court, the management team's defense includes firstly, collecting a data base to justify terminating this person if they did not modify their inappropriate conduct, and secondly, providing a data base to support the actions taken to reduce staff dissension/turnover due to the miscreant's devious ploys which disrupts the daily staff morale.

Implementing The Structured Intervention Strategy

1. Existing organization policies/procedures and code of conduct regulations should be rigorously analysed by the expert(s), a management representative(s) and team members from the "front line" to identify perceived loopholes that need to be changed or eliminated. This is a major priority in action planning and risk analysis;
2. The individual identified as a *potential* organization miscreant should be initially evaluated using the Psychopathy Spectrum

Test as a staff evaluation of the individual, using its protocol described in Chapter Three. Subsequently, the quantitative data from the test scores from the pre-determined chosen staff is collated. The results are then provided the designated expert(s), to review and proceed with a far more rigorous clinical/forensic evaluation, utilizing both qualitative and quantitative data (e.g., structured interview format; Psychopathy Spectrum Test; B-Scan 360 mentioned in Chapter 5);

3. Devise a method whereby management and the general staff attempt to align the organization miscreant's need for self-gratification with the organization's values (i.e., policy and procedures, code of conduct). This should be done in an effort to modify the organization miscreant's behavior over time. Reinforcement scheduling (see previous section) can then be introduced;

4. Team building with the staff by providing in-service training regarding the modus operandi of the organization miscreant can often *reduce* potential victimization. This process can be combined with teaching stress management techniques to reduce the staff members' potential for developing depression and anxiety, as a result of being the recipient of vindictive conduct. This behavior by the organization miscreant is often initiated very subtly, but with time can develop into an aggressive form of retaliation and condescension. For example, they might target a "problem" employee causing trouble for them. Consequently, the individual will be targeted for elimination by the organization miscreant, using any/all methods at their disposal! I have observed this type of ruthless conduct many times over the years, in a myriad of different work settings.

5. Lastly, company policy must be put into place to identify and aggressively deal with this conniving individual and their ruthless conduct. As stated by Clarke (2005, p. 264) in his identification of the aforementioned presenting behavior:

Handling (the organization miscreant) is a difficult proposition at best because they do not want 'help' to improve their behavior. For them, life and work are all about self-gratification. They have absolutely no reason to change their behavior because people are not happy with the way they are acting. They continue to use their tactics to have the person or people who are criticizing them suffer from extreme levels of stress and (which can cause) eventual 'nervous breakdown.'

In the writer's professional experience, traditional talk therapy has *little impact* on these individuals! The behavior intervention reinforcement approach described above may have some positive effect, if properly implemented by a determined and resolute team approach. Of note: One-on-one aggressive confrontation with this individual is frankly a "set-up" situation, designed to fail in most cases, leaving you open to your adversary's "tool kit" of vengeful, retaliatory behavior! Don't antagonize them by playing "hero." It requires a team approach to defeat these individuals in the majority of circumstances!

CHAPTER FIVE:

Survival Techniques to Preserve Quality of Work Life

Throughout the past four chapters I have repeatedly demonstrated how "ripe" a work environment is for the organization miscreant to exploit opportunities and impugn colleagues to achieve devious ends. All of which is done in order for them to seize the opportunity to become more entrenched in the organization's power structure! You, your most important benefactor in life, have to be VERY wary of the ways and means your particular organization can be exploited by this cold-blooded individual. That being stated, the following sections detail coping strategies to help you survive at your worksite. The writer has incorporated information reviewed from several noted experts (e.g., Babiak, Clarke, Dutton, Simon) to provide the broadest base of knowledge when interpreting the organization miscreant's behavior. More in-depth reading of these authors is located in the references section of this book. *Please take advantage of this and review the breadth and depth of knowledge provided by these experts.*

While reading Chapter Five, try to identify and position the various ploys used by these individuals, to gain authority and power within a unionized, private, or not-for-profit organization. In most circumstances, the style of management in these work milieus incorporate: a rigid, top-down unilateral chain-of-command structure; a policy and procedure protocol of the organization; ongoing staff management procedures; quality control and quality improvement protocol; in-house customer satisfaction (employees) protocol; and external customer satisfaction (business clientele) protocol. All of which are scrupulously examined and increasingly exploited over time by the organization miscreant. Their major goal is attaining power and control to meet basic unfulfilled needs, as stated previously (see Dutton, 1998, Chapter Three of this book).

All of the survival techniques mentioned in Chapter Five may help to *reduce and cushion* the effect of the trauma caused by the organization miscreant's cruel behavior. The symptoms may occur while the organization miscreant is currently employed, or long after their departure from the organization. There is often long-term emotional suppression and/or "acting out" behavior by the victims of this individual's maligning conduct, which in many cases cause simple, secondary, and complex trauma for the victims and their family members.

Set-ups

Successful Interventions with a Miscreant Boss, Co-worker, or Subordinate

The writer has provided additional information to support the following sections from Babiak et al., 2006 "Snakes in Suits: When Psychopaths Go To Work" please take the opportunity to review their book.

Boss: At most worksites the organization is expected to take the side of your boss regarding disagreements over your performance. The best defense is ALWAYS perform to your potential and complete the tasks assigned to you, unless they are illegal, unethical, or violate safety or security procedures (Babiak et al., 2006). Be open about your performance and ask for regular feedback; if this is not forthcoming, you've got a problem. Is it that simple, you ask? Absolutely, it is your *legal right* to know where you stand regarding your work performance!

The writers suggests you ask for this a minimum of twice annually, and short-term and long-term goals should be included in the report. PLEASE keep detailed logs of any *challenges* by the organization miscreant regarding these requests. It is also important to respond to this information within a twenty-four hour period. In many jurisdictions this is a legal requirement for your critique to be accepted in a court of law.

Next, always complete and submit a written memo (yes, in writing) to a boss you're worried has the presenting behavior of an organization miscreant; this memo reflects your understanding of their directive. More specifically, the memo entails discussing your understanding of what exactly it is you have been requested to do, the timetable, the assistance you expect from your co-workers (e.g., boss, peers, subordinates).

Ask to meet with your boss to review your requests and keep a personal copy of the documents SAVING his written responses to your requests. Don't be surprised if the miscreant challenges your requests, stalls in providing data you've requested, or is generally contrary to your requests. They can become very concerned about "hidden motives" as you are *not* presenting as a submissive personality (by providing *boundary-specific* behavior).

In essence, come to these meetings with several solutions that you have developed and assess as reasonable options. The organization miscreant hopefully views this initiative as you being a results-oriented employee, yet wants to achieve a mutually agreed-upon goal. The next suggestion may appear counter-intuitive, but if you can, build a reasonable working relationship with your boss, hard as it may seem. Why you ask?

PLEASE REMEMBER: at this point your boss "holds the cards" and has the power and authority to make your life/work miserable! Regardless, this request is a *work in progress* and can be a hard one to achieve, to put it mildly! Conversely, appearing less than forthright, and worse, argumentative with these individuals is a recipe for disaster—you have to play this one very carefully! Why you ask? As stated previously, these individuals have learned and carried out this malevolent behavior since early adolescence in many cases and are immensely practiced in assessment of micro, macro, and mega elements of the work force. More to the point, I was told back in the 1970s, "I seldom lose with rank amateurs, or anyone else for that matter." Unfortunately, he was right!

Co-worker: With a co-worker deemed untrustworthy and/or ruthless with a manipulative bent, build open and honest relationships with your colleagues, follow policy/procedures, and if you're required to work closely with this individual, don't fall into the trap of doing their work for them! To get these predators off your back you will often be tempted (or pressured) to capitulate. Colluding with them is a BIG mistake: you will likely be "done in" politically when you're no longer useful and most often used to mask their poor work performance. As mentioned previously, aggressive confrontation with this miscreant can be dangerous, as it will undoubtedly be manipulated, "spin doctored" in lay terminology, as you being the instigator of the problem, not them.

As often stated in the book, they have learned and become VERY adept at charm, manipulation, and guile. If you think you can defeat them over time, good luck, they can rip your heart out (if threatened by your strengths) by way of underhanded behavior! Your career and means of making a living to support your family should be on your mind at all times during impromptu collaborations and the subsequent interactions/circumstances which follow. They usually occur in a "lock-step" manner, which you will come to recognize over time dealing with the organization miscreant.

Specifically, your attempts at one-on-one confrontation are a policy of action with good intentions but are often twisted by the miscreant to meet their needs/desires, after carefully assessing your motive and nature of request. BE CAREFUL and listen to your intuitive side before taking action. We will discuss coping strategies later on in much greater detail.

Subordinate: Organizational miscreants, if you hadn't already guessed, rarely make good subordinates! Their tendency to lie, manipulate, and use charm as a method of enticement is reflected in "the end justifies the means" rationale. This is the antithesis of an ideal colleague, don't you think!

When you're around a subordinate who you feel is an organization miscreant, use the following techniques to "cushion" the impact of their negative behavior:

1. Be very careful about boundaries; they have a tendency to collect and use information against you with the pretence of developing a solid, working relationship;
2. Try to remain in control, as you will be emotionally challenged by their unsavory, clever ploys to manipulate you;
3. Be aware that the organization miscreant's description of a situation is often fabricated, with omissions of very important detail. Do not take at face value what they state actually happened, or the manner in which they state it happened;
4. Keep written notation of your interactions with subordinate organization miscreants. Time has a habit of interfering with memory accuracy. As stated previously, maintain a written account completed *no later* than twenty-four hours post conversation (legal requirement in many jurisdictions) meeting, this document can be worth its weight in gold AND be a job or career saver!
5. Lastly, if you are intimidated by a miscreant—which can happen daily—shift your gaze to their EYEBROWS. Don't worry, they will not be able to recognize you not giving them eye contact. You will find your fear is much reduced, as miscreants often use menacing stares to intimidate. Try the eyebrow technique, it works wonders!
6. Last but not least, complete the Psychopathy Spectrum Test on these individuals to ease your mind. Using a lay evaluation test such as the Psychopathy Spectrum Test to collect quantitative data can provide enormous support or challenge against your intuitive suspicions. The test is less than thirty minutes of your time.

Cons and Other Nefarious Activities

The tactics and strategies of the organization miscreant are subtle and developed in stages (Babiak & Hare, 2019, pp. 288-295). The writer has provided additional information supporting the Babiak et al. material.

In the early stages, they complete a micro then macro analysis of the organization, its policies and procedures, and the behavior of the employee constituents, ostensibly asking themselves what operational style they must utilize to fulfill self-gratifying needs, and how effectively will their behavior be detected by their colleagues and the management system in place? Most importantly, from the beginning they examine their colleagues' weaknesses in order to exploit them in the future when the time arises. Subsequently, the organization's rules and protocol being learned and absorbed by miscreants are subtly challenged then violated.

With time, colleagues become *desensitized* to this odd "testy" behavior, and if the organization miscreants are confronted about their unsavory conduct, they will plead ignorance and attribute their behavior to being new in the organization. They will often request another assignment "to prove their worth." Unfortunately, this usually includes one caveat—that the job requires little staff interaction; please keep this in mind! This allows greater opportunity for victimizing without being detected, as the manipulator's job function in this new role does *not* require close working relationships with their colleagues.

As progress occurs in time, the organization miscreant's detailed knowledge of the rules and regulations of the worksite increases their ability to talk their way out of compromising situations when complaints start "rolling in." As stated in Chapter Four, they become VERY ADEPT at covering up their mistakes, transgressions, and overt errors. Keep the following in mind as well! They increase their expertise at challenging the protocol at all levels of the organization's infrastructure, but most importantly, they become adept at identifying weaknesses of individuals ("marks") within the work environment and exploiting them. This often includes "scapegoating" feuding colleagues, as stated in Chapter Four, who are used as "dupes" in the miscreant's political endeavours to rise to the top of the organization.

Do they worry about getting caught? Yes and no. Their narcissistic personality traits, which include grandiosity and self-entitlement, interfere with insight. Remember, they are lacking in empathy with little conscience about the consequence of their actions to others, which allows the calculated exploitation of their colleagues. The ability to learn and exploit any situation to meet their needs has been developed and refined to such a degree that the potential for error is much reduced, relative to the normal employee's perception accuracy in these situations. Therefore, the risk of being caught, albeit low, is worth the risk of continuing to function in the same devious manner, which has become habituated and is second nature responding by the time the organization miscreant has entered the workforce. When they are eventually caught in their deceitful dealings and feel that the organization will "win" against them, they often capitulate and move on, or attempt to eliminate the complaint, using whatever unsavory means they have at their disposal (e.g., emotional blackmail, quid pro quo: "I helped you in the past, now you have to help me, *or else*" is verbalized outright or implied).

Regarding this last statement, organization miscreants have a habit of compiling dossiers on their victims that can be used against them when action is needed for basic survival at the worksite. Hollywood movies aside, this actually happens in real life, so don't be a victim!

As stated frequently in this book, organization miscreants identify vulnerable people and use the power of knowledge of the system, its operational protocol, and identified weaknesses to target and exploit their colleagues. Clarke (2005) states the key factors miscreants look for include a victim's vulnerability, low self-esteem, desire to change, and a yearning for a better life. Consequently, a systemic approach entwining their victim's behavior is devised, which entails the following paradigm of exploitation:

1. The organizational miscreant frequently begins by breaking the victim's confidence, making the individual fearful of challenging the miscreant's behavior towards them. To reinforce how serious the intention is, confrontation and intimidation ploys are "acted out" against the victim numerous times. This maintains the "top dog-bottom dog" relationship, which over time crushes the incentive to initiate any retaliation, thereby causing learned helplessness.

2. This behavior establishes the consequence of challenging the miscreant's authority, and once fear is established the miscreant "tweaks" the relationship any time they feel the victim is losing their "bottom dog" position; thus the fear and control is maintained and the victimization persists.

In conjunction, the organization miscreant usually pushes colleagues away from the "mark," isolating the individual by impugning their sense of worth and ability to achieve success without the "support" of the organization miscreant. Typically, this bullying and manipulative conduct eventually reduces the victim's self-esteem, allowing the miscreant to better meet their need for power and control. Remember, the lack of conscience by miscreants allows them to feel little to no remorse regarding their transgressions with the victimized colleague OR ANYONE ELSE for that matter!

So, if you get that intuitive "gut" feeling about Mr./Ms. Niceness at the office, after they increase the over-stepping of boundaries with you, they could be initiating an exploitation scenario with serious negative consequences for your emotional health and professional reputation!

Think about it; your career is the means by which you make a living, and your mental health is a precious commodity and not to be tampered with.

Problematic Behaviors Indicating Trouble Lies Ahead

The following is a list of behaviors identified by Babiak et al. (2006). The writer includes this valuable section with supplemental information and reiterates the suggestion to review expert opinion from the various authors mentioned and referenced in this book.

Problematic behaviors are often observed in clusters and initiated by the organization miscreant and include:

a. *Inability to form a team* – the organization miscreant is unable to form a workable team. More specifically, they find fraternizing, "teaming up" with colleagues whom they view as adversaries very difficult. In conjunction, the organization miscreant withholds and distorts information to the detriment of the team and habitually disrupts the homeostasis (i.e., balance) of the team. They are highly competitive people who frequently attack, berate, and denigrate! In conjunction, they can't take directives unless it suits their purpose, they dominate and bully—we've heard that one before, haven't we;

b. *Inability to share* – their personality style requires them to work parasitically. Specifically, they don't like to share the credit where it's due. Organization miscreants tend to "keep out of the loop." They will provide information when it suits their purpose and with an ulterior motive;

c. *Disparate treatment of staff* – disparate treatment of "marks" is often subtle and very often only known to the victim. Subsequently, the victim's passive behavior disallows forthright action to be taken by management, which could rectify the problem if management knew about the problem earlier;

d. *Inability to tell the truth* – organization miscreants are pathological liars, and because they don't manifest guilt in doing so, they habitually cross over from truth to lies and no one knows the real story for a very long time. Questioning their integrity is inviting RETRIBUTION with a capital R;

e. *Inability to be modest* – the organization miscreant's continuum in this context ranges from immodesty to arrogance and the *consistency of this behavior* on a day-to-day basis is what is most often identified by their co-workers. In a sentence, there is no such thing as genuine modesty among organization miscreants;

f. *Inability to accept blame* – organization miscreants rarely take responsibility for their actions, in fact they tend to project the blame onto their colleagues, which identifies to a "T" active instrumental aggression (i.e., when an individual intentionally acts aggressively to achieve a particular purpose— there is no emotional drive) as opposed to hostile (i.e., emotional) aggression;

g. *Inability to act predictably* – organization miscreants are inconsistent and tend to disrupt and embarrass with irrational behavior often acting as a "loose cannon" at their place of employment, but *not* usually in front of superiors;

h. *Inability to react calmly* – in conjunction with (g), organization miscreants are frequently unable to act calmly and rationally when faced with a crisis or under pressure. In general, and when out of corporate visibility, organization miscreants frequently display over-reactive behavior, or, in lay terminology, become "drama queens" when faced with these circumstances. The effect of this outlandish behavior is a reduction of team cohesion/ morale, and because senior management is *not* there to witness the behavior, it may continue for a very long time and lastly;

i. *Inability to act without aggression* – as stated, organization miscreants are masters of manipulation; intimidation, and coercion!! Direct, "in-your-face" bullying can be a major presenting feature of these individuals. Those who intervene, be it on a supervisory level, management, or consultants, do so at the risk of being sued or at least threatened with litigation! As stated, many times in this book, organization miscreants are scheming, intelligent (street smart), and ruthless! This fact I hope is crystallized in your brain by now, it is important to be aware of the power they think they possess (at your expense).

The miscreant has evaluated the organization's strengths and needs and will challenge the source of their discomfort with a retinue of "ammunition" regarding organization failures, shortcomings, etcetera, to defend their actions (rationalization). The presenting aggression, both active and passive, has to be seen to be believed and has, in my professional experience, caused many a senior manager to "squirm" in their boots! It's a "game" and miscreants are masters if not grand master chess players instigating this very ruthless and destructive game. Metaphors aside and for your future well-being, BE VERY CAREFULL when interacting with this human replicant!

How to Challenge Delinquent Behavior by the Organization Miscreant

A number of excellent coping strategies (Simon 2010) have been identified to keep in mind when involved with an organization miscreant. The following protocols should provide you with a greater sense of personal empowerment:

a. *Accept no excuses* – Don't accept rationalizations for the organization miscreant's inappropriate, aggressive conduct! Simply don't accept their rationale; it is totally irrelevant. The "bottom line" is don't accept or be influenced by any excuses they offer for their conduct;

b. *Judge actions not intentions* – Judge the behavior itself; remember, organization miscreants are brilliant at impression-management. Behavior patterns from the organization miscreant provide the information you require about their character—observe and appraise THE BEHAVIOR, and be careful in doing so;

c. *Set personal limits* – Know your personal boundaries and what you'll accept or not accept from a colleague before you take some counter-measure. As well, what is the level of confrontation you're prepared to make in order to defend yourself? Identify your personal boundaries or risk exploitation at the hands of a very shrewd and ruthless manipulator;

d. *Make direct requests* – Use "I" statements and avoid generalities. Make clear your boundaries with the miscreant, which influences reduced distortion regarding what you expect from them. If their response is not clear to your direct request, you may be set up in a "top-dog - bottom-dog" relationship— BEWARE and BE CAUTIOUS;

e. *Accept only direct responses* – As an adjunct to (d), insist on clear, direct answers, respectfully assert yourself, and expect a forthright response. Answers that are exaggerated, understated, or "masked" suggest they are attempting to manipulate you;

f. *Stay focused in the present* – Watch out for diversionary and evasive behavior from the organization miscreant. Stay in the "here and now"; their willingness to change as a result of the point you're making of the confrontation will give you an indication of how flexible they are in modifying their behavior towards you! In essence, do they change their tactics as a result of your confrontation, and do you really care at this point— hopefully not, but it's your choice;

g. *When confronting aggressive behavior by the miscreant, keep the responsibility on the aggressor* – Specifically, the focus of your statement should be on what the miscreant did to injure your self-esteem. Don't be sucked into their attempts to rationalize and shift blame. Ignore their rationalizations and continue your questioning using the "broken record" technique (repeating the point) most of us learned in assertiveness training. Keep the focus on the miscreant changing a specific behavior that has impugned your integrity; they usually try to "slip and slide" out of any responsibility for their actions. WATCH OUT FOR THIS MANEUVER;

h. *When you confront, avoid sarcasm, hostility, and demeaning behavior* – Organization miscreants construe any kind of confrontation as a CHALLENGE, which precipitates an attack, and ATTACK they will! Generally, as stated before, they project blame, deny and rationalize to avoid responsibility for their inappropriate behavior. Consequently, you should assert in a steady "off the shoulder," non-aggressive manner, and simply identify the manipulator's inappropriate behavior. Remember, confrontation *with tact* is necessary with this type of individual. It is important and vital to learn to confront tactfully and avoid aggression or denigration; it only escalates the problem at hand;

i. *Avoid making threats* – NEVER THREATEN but take action to protect yourself and achieve your needs. This is not as easy as it sounds when enticed to compete in close-quarter "combat" with this type of ruthless personality. Keep focused on a positive approach while defending your position and with practice (there is that "p" word again) it will become easier;

j. *Take action quickly* – Organization miscreants lack internal controls, as stated above. They aggressively seek out and attempt to "steamroll" to achieve their goals, at your expense. Be ready to confront their tactics and then respond in an assertive, boundary-specific manner. Get away from the "bottom-dog" position and seek a better balance of power;

k. *Speak for yourself* – If you have the courage, strength of character, and willpower, deal with the organization miscreant by yourself; don't find a "defender," as it identifies your passivity and potential for future exploitation. When you're alone with a miscreant, be assertive about what you want. This is easier said than done, but you have to start somewhere, and with practice, setting boundaries should become easier;

l. *Make reasonable agreements* – Make agreements that are "transparent" and expect this in return. Be wary of being cheated and remember the miscreant's proclivity to use guile in crafting lies to meet their needs at your expense! Try to propose as many "win-win" scenarios as you can. This tact dissipates the miscreant's tendency to compete at all costs to win and reduces the frequency of conflict! They most prefer a "win-lose" situation with you, the identified "mark," ending up in the "bottom-dog" position. They will also accept (with chagrin) a second-best option, a "win-win" result, yes, you heard it right, a "win-win" second-best option;

m. *Be prepared for consequences* – The organization miscreant WANTS TO WIN in their interactions with you and can be vindictive as hell, so prepare yourself for antagonistic behavior and take appropriate action to protect yourself. Assess the continuum of responses the miscreant might make against you, and, if possible, as stated above, clarify the miscreant's position on a one-to-one basis to show strength. As an adjunct and when necessary, involve yourself with a strong support network to decrease the miscreant's power against you. Remember: Support NETWORK, not defender—there is a big distinction;

n. *Be honest with yourself* – Know your own needs, desires, abilities, and strengths/weaknesses, because the organization miscreant will assess and attempt to "press your buttons." THAT I CAN GUARANTEE! Deceiving yourself, or better stated, deluding yourself about your strengths and needs can quickly place you in a subservient "bottom- dog" relationship with this devious and tenacious individual. KEEP AWARE of the "dance with the devil" paradigm that can play out with an organization miscreant.

In simple language, forget ego, your mental health is not worth the risk! Let me expand on this "ego thing" for a moment. Dutton (2012) has characterized the personality traits of an organization miscreant very adroitly to include: ruthlessness, charm, focus, mental toughness, fearlessness, mindfulness, and action (pp.185-86). These formidable opponents choose to apply the different personality traits depending on the circumstance they encounter, as Dutton states, "fading in and out to match the soundtrack" (p.186).

Specifically, the miscreant chooses the right trait or set of traits to match the context of the situation in which they find themselves with a "mark" and initiate their predatory behavior to meet their need for power and control. At this stage of reading the book, do you still think you can match the miscreant's cunning duplicity, single handed!? Hmm, I hope not. Please, don't tempt fate and try to prove me wrong, especially when this tyrant's "gig" is at full ram speed. Their behavior has been rehearsed, habituated, and "acted out" since adolescence in many cases, and certainly by late adolescence/early twenties is refined and pathological in nature. But there I go repeating myself.

Lastly, when the expert forensic clinician(s) have been hired by management, they will probably use an assessment instrument called the B-scan (Business Scan Long-Form) as developed by Babiak and Hare, discussed in Chapter 10 of their book *Snakes in Suits: Understanding and Surviving the Psychopaths In Your Office* (2019, pp.219-225). This assessment instrument has been developed for Human Resource departments/business consultants "to measure or predict known or suspected relationships with other variables associated with psychopathy in general" (p. 223). The authors further state, "the B-Scan is strongly associated with Narcissism and Machiavellianism, low levels of Agreeableness and Conscientiousness" which support a psychopathic presentation, and its structure reflects the four-factor Dark Tetrad mentioned throughout this book. It is a very useful assessment instrument that provides additional strength to the array of quantitative data required to defeat the organizational miscreant.

My final suggestion to enrich your quality of work life is this: Stay mentally tough, use the information provided above, and watch your boundaries like a hawk! Please take my suggestion to locate and read thoroughly the expert opinions of the authors mentioned in the book! Good luck in all future endeavors, and hopefully we'll meet one day.

Sincerely with regard,
Jake Hagerman

Author's Psychopathy Spectrum Test Results – Fifteen Vignettes

Explanation of Terms Provided by the Psychopathy Spectrum Test

Psychopaths: characterized by both the interpersonal manipulativeness and callousness of sociopaths, as well as the anger, disinhibited behavior, and emotional dysregulation of the impulsive personality. This combination of deviance, cunning, and aggression results in individuals who are truly among the most dangerous and volatile of people.

Sociopaths: characterized by interpersonal manipulativeness and deviance, as well as egocentricity, callousness, and the lack of remorse or guilt. Sociopaths are capable of employing glibness and superficial charm to cunningly use people, *but generally lack the impulsivity and overtly violent disposition of psychopaths and impulsive personalities.*

Impulsive: characterized by an angry, disinhibited, and thoughtless attitude towards life, as well as a pattern of negative emotionality and emotional dysregulation. They frequently resort to bullying, intimidation, and social aggression when frustrated, but lack the cunning manipulativeness of sociopaths and psychopaths.

Normal: characterized by low scores on both dimensions of the psychopathy spectrum (social deviance and impulsive aggression).

However, please note that someone who is "normal" on the psychopathy spectrum may still have other personality maladaptive qualities, or generalized inclinations towards anger.

The writer's evaluation is based on first hand involvement with most of the individuals identified in the Vignettes, or from descriptors of these individuals from colleagues employed or formerly employed in the field of mental health. The test responses are my personal opinion of each individual's presenting features either witnessed first-hand or described by a clinically trained colleague with an advanced post graduate degree(s). The writer and his colleagues are qualified in the use of psychological testing (psychometric evaluation), including personality assessment.

> VIGNETTE 1 – *Sven* scored: 68.75 percent sociopathic; 63.64 percent impulsive; 41.33 percent more psychopathic than the population average.

> VIGNETTE 2 – *Sharon "Twenty-year-old blonde"* scored: 98.44 percent sociopathic; 86.36 percent impulsive; 67.53 percent more psychopathic than the population average.

> VIGNETTE 3 – *Joe "Administrator/Director/Autocrat"* scored: 79.69 percent sociopathic; 40.91 percent impulsive; 35.43 percent more psychopathic than the population average.

> VIGNETTE 4 – *Ned "the lead pipe cinch"* scored: 89.06 sociopathic; 75.00 percent impulsive; 57.16 percent more psychopathic than the population average.

> VIGNETTE 5 – *Nina "The Cretin business partner"* scored: 78.13 percent sociopathic; 56.82 percent impulsive; 42.6 percent more psychopathic than the population average.

> VIGNETTE 6 (*cont'd from Vignette 5*) – Nina*"The Cretin-former business partner"* scored: 78.13 percent

sociopathic; 56.82 percent impulsive; 42.61 percent more psychopathic than the population average (no change in behavior).

VIGNETTE 7 – *Casey "Second-in-Command"* scored: 71.88 percent sociopathic; 45.45 percent impulsive; 33.80 percent more psychopathic than the population average.

VIGNETTE 8 – *George "the Executive Director"* scored: 78.13 percent sociopathic; 52.27 percent Impulsive, 40.33 percent more psychopathic than the population average.

VIGNETTE 9 – *Gazlen* scored: 84.38 percent sociopathic; 63.64 percent impulsive; 49.14 percent more psychopathic than the population average.

VIGNETTE 10 – *Macabeus* scored: 98.44 percent sociopathic; 84.09 percent impulsive; 66.40 percent more psychopathic than the population average.

VIGNETTE 11 – *Mr. Bogus Professional* scored: 89.06 percent sociopathic; 45.45 percent impulsive; 42.39 percent more psychopathic than the population average.

VIGNETTE 12 – *The Gentleman Hockey Player* scored: 81.25 percent sociopathic; 43.18 percent impulsive; 37.35 percent more psychopathic than the population average.

VIGNETTE 13 – *Fred* scored: 73.44 percent sociopathic; 61.36 percent impulsive; 42.53 percent more psychopathic than the population average.

VIGNETTE 14 – *Dybuk* scored: 87.50 percent sociopathic; 63.64 percent impulsive; 50.70 percent more psychopathic than the population average.

VIGNETTE 15 – *The Interrogator* scored: 89.06 percent sociopathic; 56.82 percent impulsive; 48.07 percent more psychopathic than the population average.

Average Scores for the Fifteen Candidates

SOCIOPATHY	83.37 percent
IMPULSIVE	60.13 percent
PSYCHOPATHY	45.03 percent[6]

Keeping that in mind, the average score of the fifteen candidates was 45 percent *more* psychopathic than the population average, this is a *very significant statistic*. Management beware!

---

6   This subscale is measured differently than the sociopathy and impulsive subscales.

EPILOGUE

This is my third book discussing organization miscreant behavior. The initial text was entitled *Love Your Enemies in Case Your Friends Turn Out to be Bastards: Organizational Case Studies Examining Worksite Politics* (2014); the second book, *Sharks, Slimeballs, and Malcontents: Organizational Survival Guide* (2022); and now, *Ruthless Predators: Miscreants in the Workplace and How to Deal with Them (2024)*. Why the corny titles, you ask? Primarily to catch the eye of a bookstore browser who is searching for more advanced information on the subject is the answer—but also the book is written in plain English! Nothing "fancy dancy," nope, just the facts and a review of fifteen vignettes which occurred from the early-mid 1970s to as recently as 2019.

I introduced the vignette analysis as a training process, to enable the reader to become more adept at assessing behavior that may reflect the Dark Tetrad. The risk analysis-evaluation process should help twig your antenna to full alert when encountering behavior that reflects the Dark Tetrad symptomatology in your work environment. I would also suggest you periodically review some or all (your choice) of the vignettes to keep you attuned to this type of psychopathology, at the very least to hone your skill set, and for safety reasons, as you travel from job to job.

Why write three books with the corny titles repeating the same message? To be honest, the one *major* event that sent me on this noteworthy journey was the Bernie Madoff disgrace. He is technically a *corporate* psychopath; nevertheless, it ignited a myriad of conflicting emotions in me, watching the line-ups of victimized clientele who had believed in the man's "blah blah" subterfuge, and had been, in many cases, financially devastated (nineteen billion dollars defrauded over forty years)!

The *second event* was less dramatic but allowed the introspection to percolate, as I state below:

These predators routinely abuse quality of life and work life, through playing a game of cause-effect predation (enjoying the power and control it provides at another person's expense). Unfortunately, they have refined this vicious game to near perfection, which is hard to defeat, as I observed over many decades this cat-and-mouse ruthlessness, first as a naïve beginner- practitioner, then as a "shop-worn" qualified clinician. This eventually led to consulting positions in a variety of work environments. The personalities of the organization miscreants were different, but the Dark Tetrad remained the same. In essence, these two motivators activated my gut reaction, which ignited an action plan, essentially, "Why don't you write about your personal experiences (under an assumed name for safety/protection) as a potential worksite resource, and for victimized people who have been traumatized?"

And let's not forget the family members that suffer secondary trauma as a result of the organization miscreant's cruel, cold-blooded behavior to the identified victim. The torment of observing the ongoing suffering of their loved one being harassed and demeaned was and is profoundly disturbing!

All of this energized me to write about my experiences and provide a knowledge base for the general population to absorb and increase their survival ability when encountering this human wrecking ball!

Once again, sincerely with regard,
Jake

REFERENCES

Babiak, P. (1995). "When psychopaths go to work: A case study of an industrial psychopath", *Applied Psychology: An International Review*, Vol. 44, 171-188.

Babiak, P. & Hare, R.D. (2006). *Snakes in Suits: When Psychopaths go to Work*. New York, NY: Harper Business.

Babiak, P. & Hare, R.D (2019). *Snakes in Suits: Understanding and Surviving the Psychopaths in your Office*. New York, NY: Harper Business.

Burnam, B.R. (1995). *Evaluating Human Resources, Programs, and Organizations*. Malabar, FL: Krieger Publishing Company.

Clarke, J. (2005). *Working with Monsters: How to Identify and Protect Yourself from the Workplace Psychopath*. Sydney, Australia: Random House.

Cleckley, H.M. (1976). *The Mask of Sanity* (5th Ed.) St. Louis: Mosby, (original work published in 1941).

Diagnostic Statistical Manual of Mental Disorders (2022): (Fifth ed. Text Rev.) *DSM-TM* 5 American Psychiatric Association. Washington, DC.

Dutton, D.G. (1998). *Violence and Control in Intimate Relationships: The Abusive Personality.* New York, NY: The Guilford Press.

Dutton, D.G. (2012). *The Wisdom of Psychopaths: What Saints, Spies, and Serial Killers can Teach Us about Success.* Toronto, Canada: Doubleday.

Hagerman J. (2014). *Love your Enemies: In Case Your Friends Turn Out to be Bastards: Organizational Case Studies Examining Worksite Politics.* Inkwater Press. USA.

Hagerman J. (2021). *Sharks, Slimeballs, and Malcontents: Organizational Survival Guide.* Self-published.

IDR-PST Labs International (2022). *The Psychopathy Spectrum Test.* Based on the research of Michael R. Levenson but is not associated with Levenson and is not the equivalent of the Levenson Self-Report Psychopathy Test. The Psychopathy Spectrum Test is a scientifically-validated instrument for measuring a person's degree of psychopathy. It is used to assess psychopathic traits in non-institutional people. https://www.idrlabs.com/psychopathy-spectrum/test.php

Levenson, M; Kiehl, K.; Fitzpatrick, C. (1995). "Assessing psychopathic attributes in a non-institutionalized population". *Journal of Personality and Social Psychology*, 68, 151-158.

Moshagen, M., Hilbig, B.E., & Zettler, I. (2018). "The dark core of personality". *Psychological Review.* 125(5), 656-688.

Simon, G. (2010). *In Sheep's Clothing: Understanding and Dealing with Manipulative People* (2nd Ed.). Pankhurst Brothers Publishers, Inc.

www.ingramcontent.com/pod-product-compliance
Lightning Source LLC
Chambersburg PA
CBHW051431280526
45785CB00003B/1242